AWESOME ANIMALS

&

AMAZING ANIMALS

COLORING BOOK
2 BOOK BUNDLE

AWESOME ANIMALS
Coloring Book

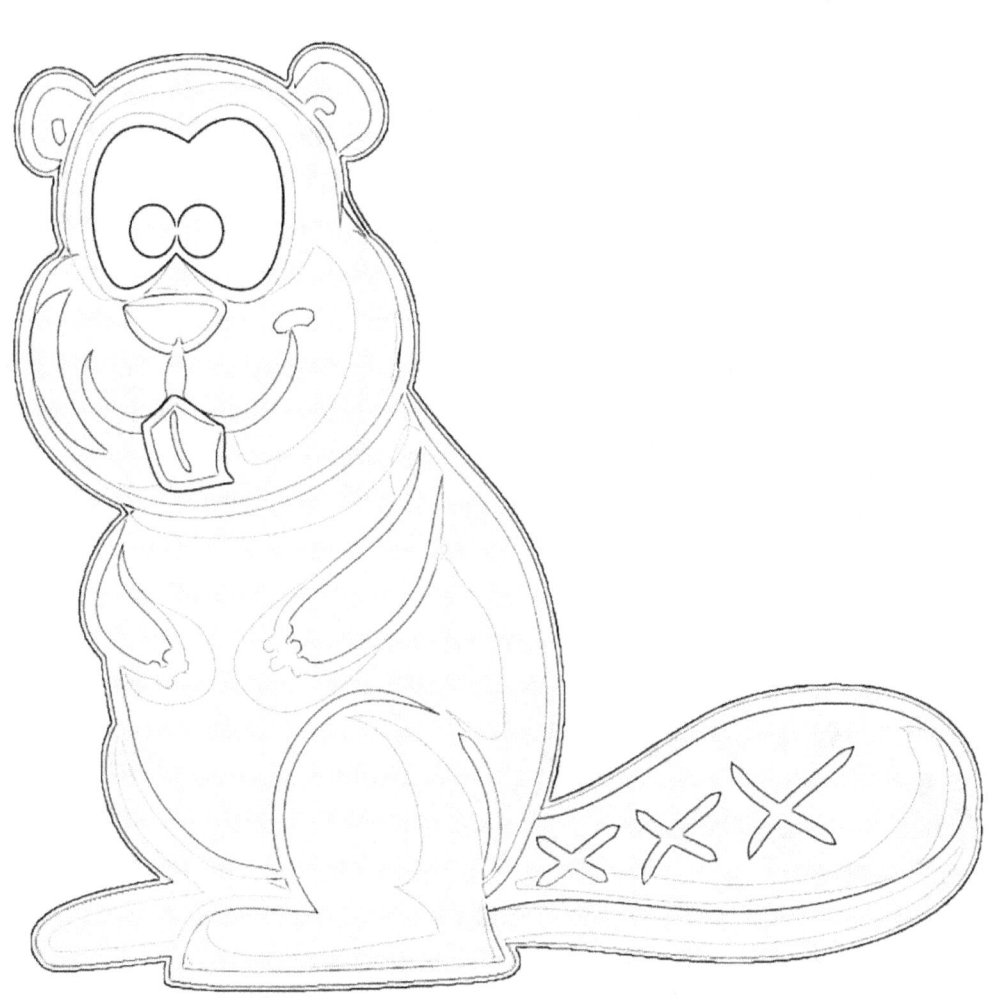

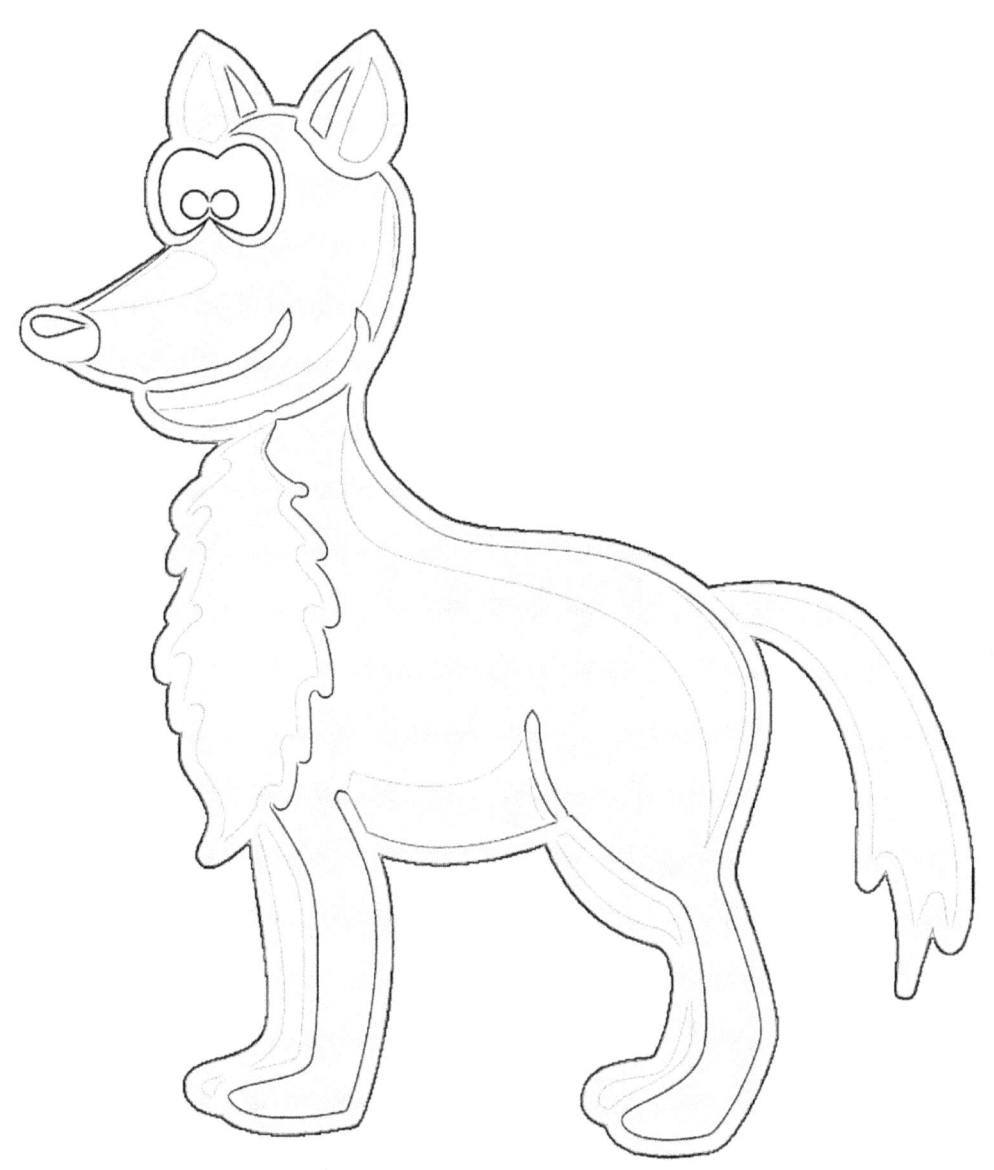

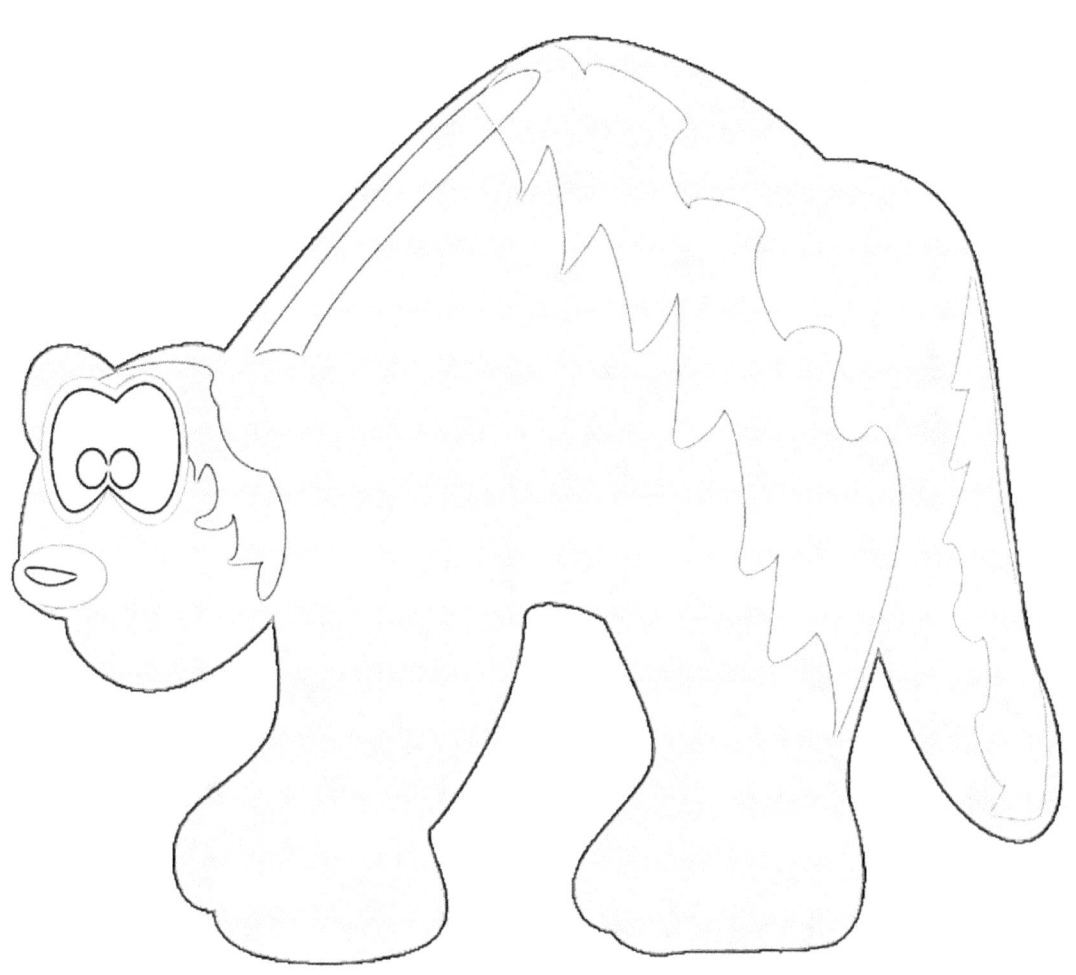

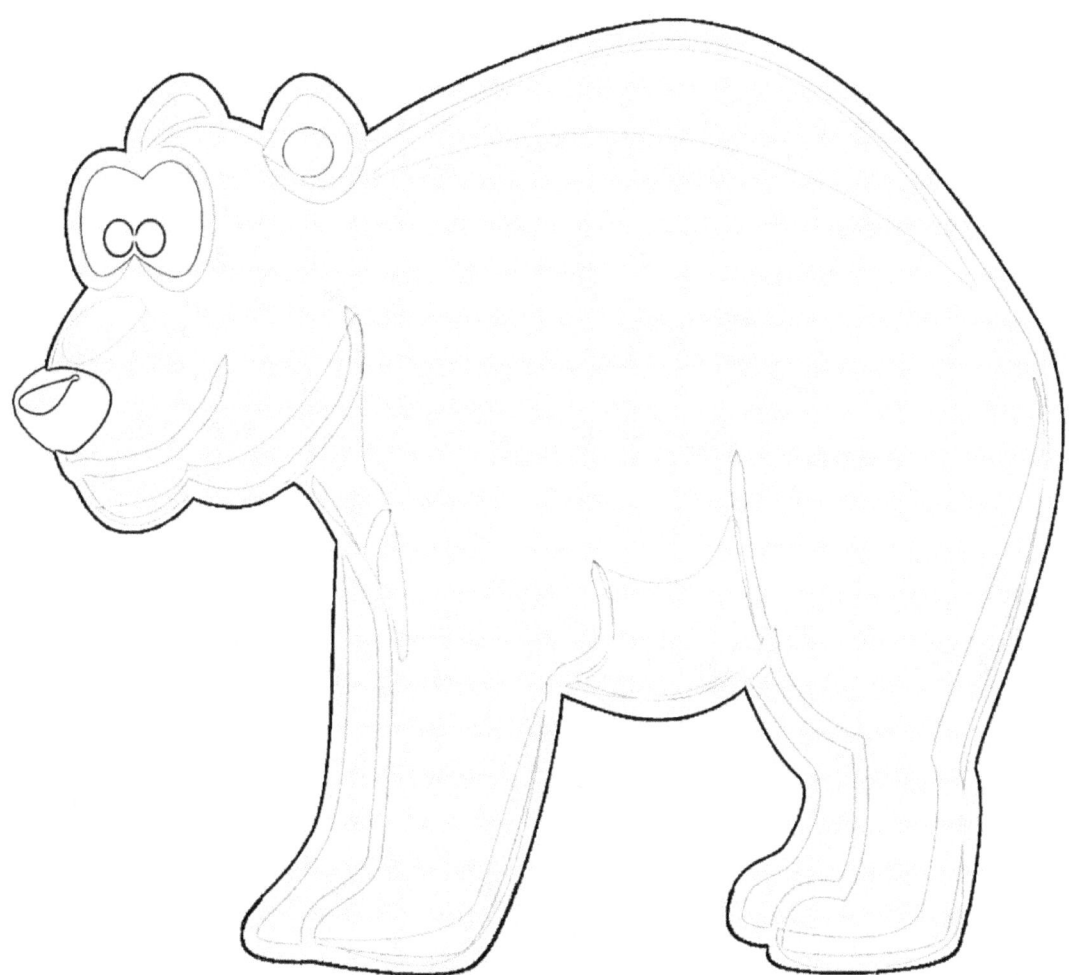

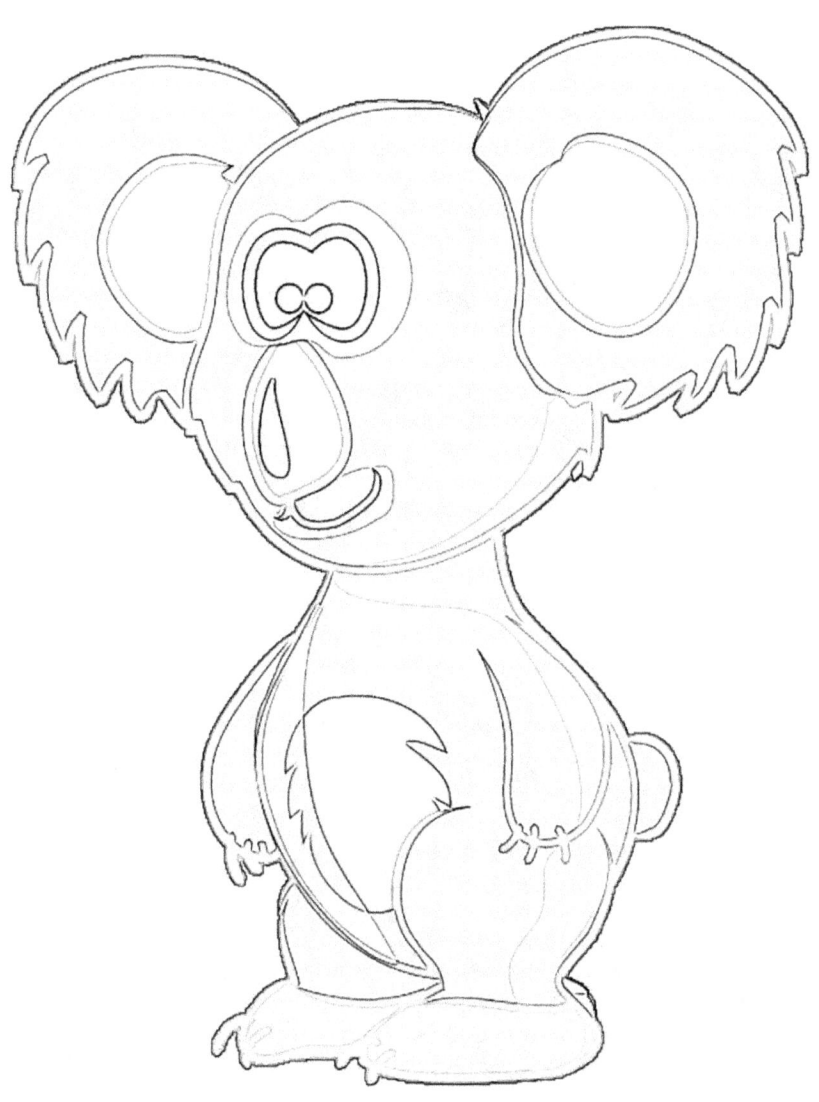

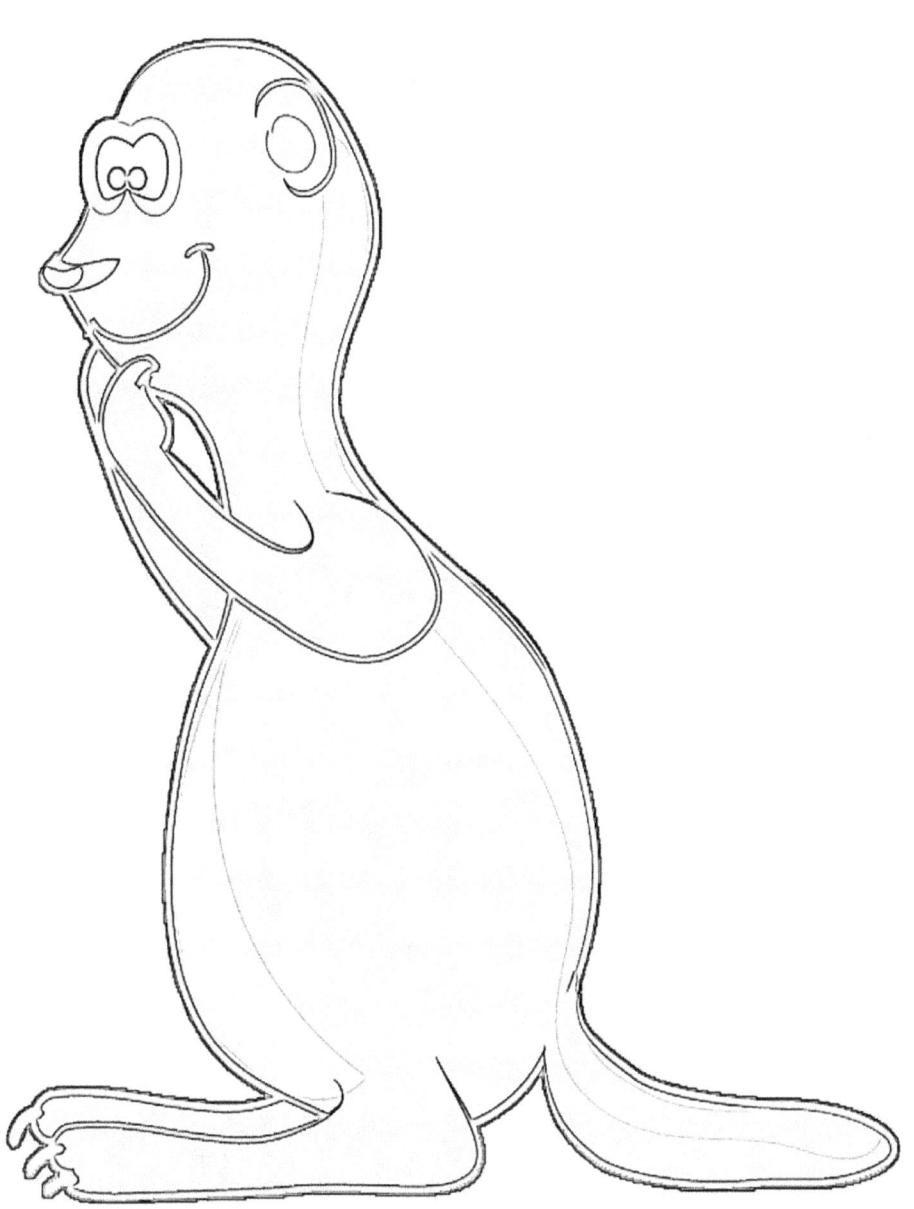

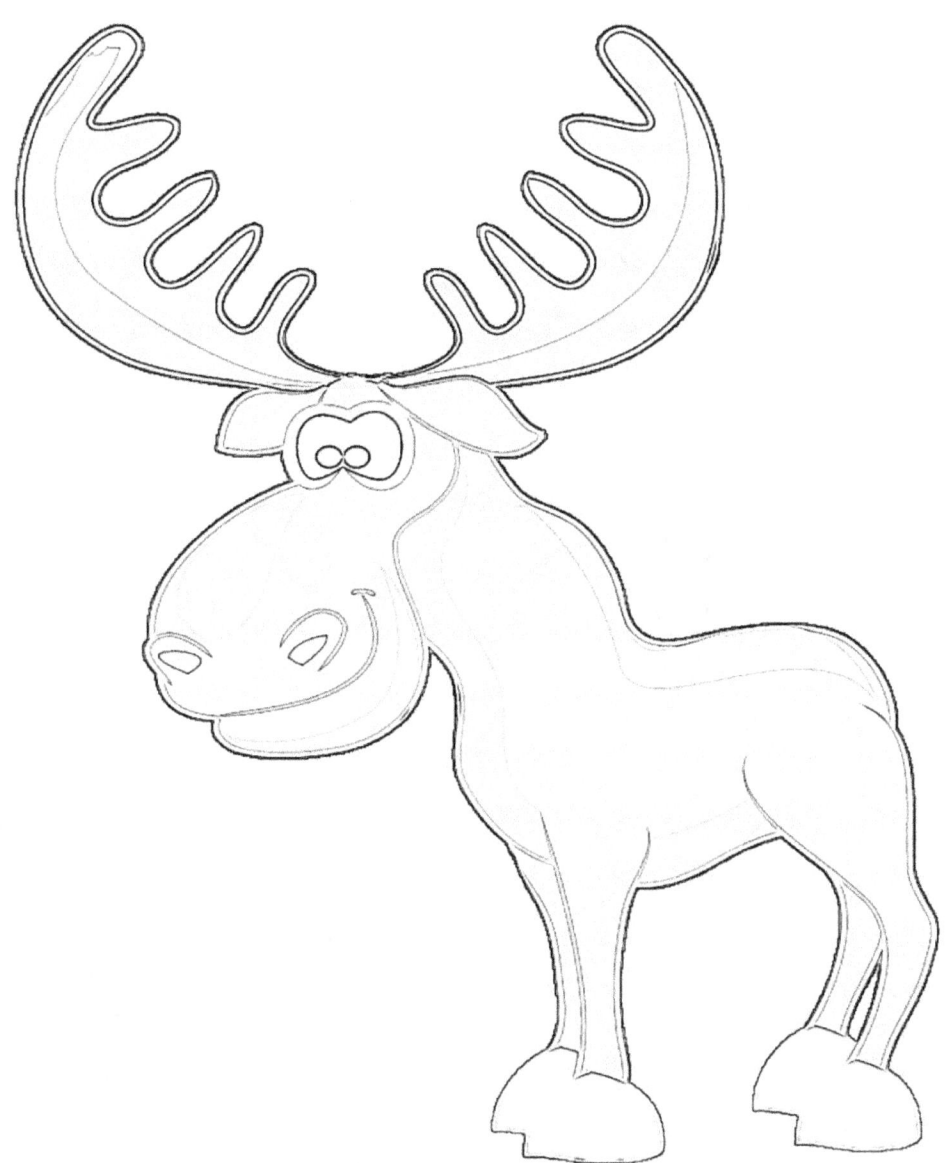

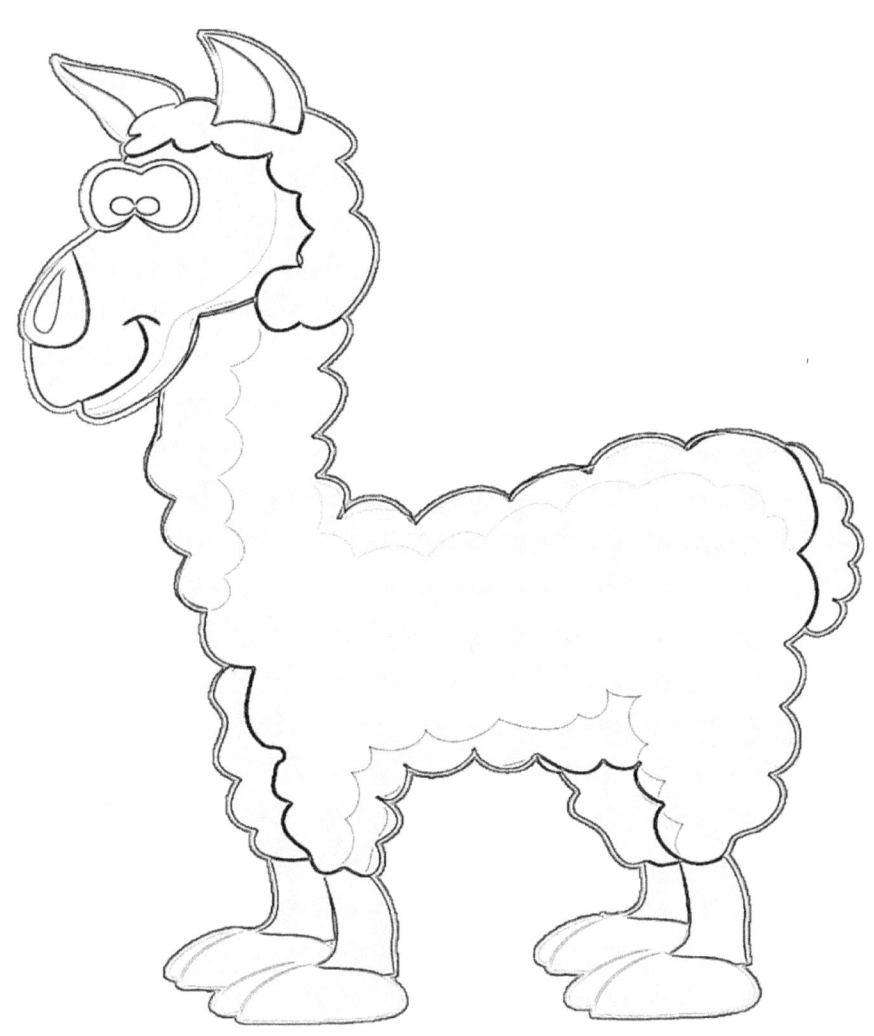

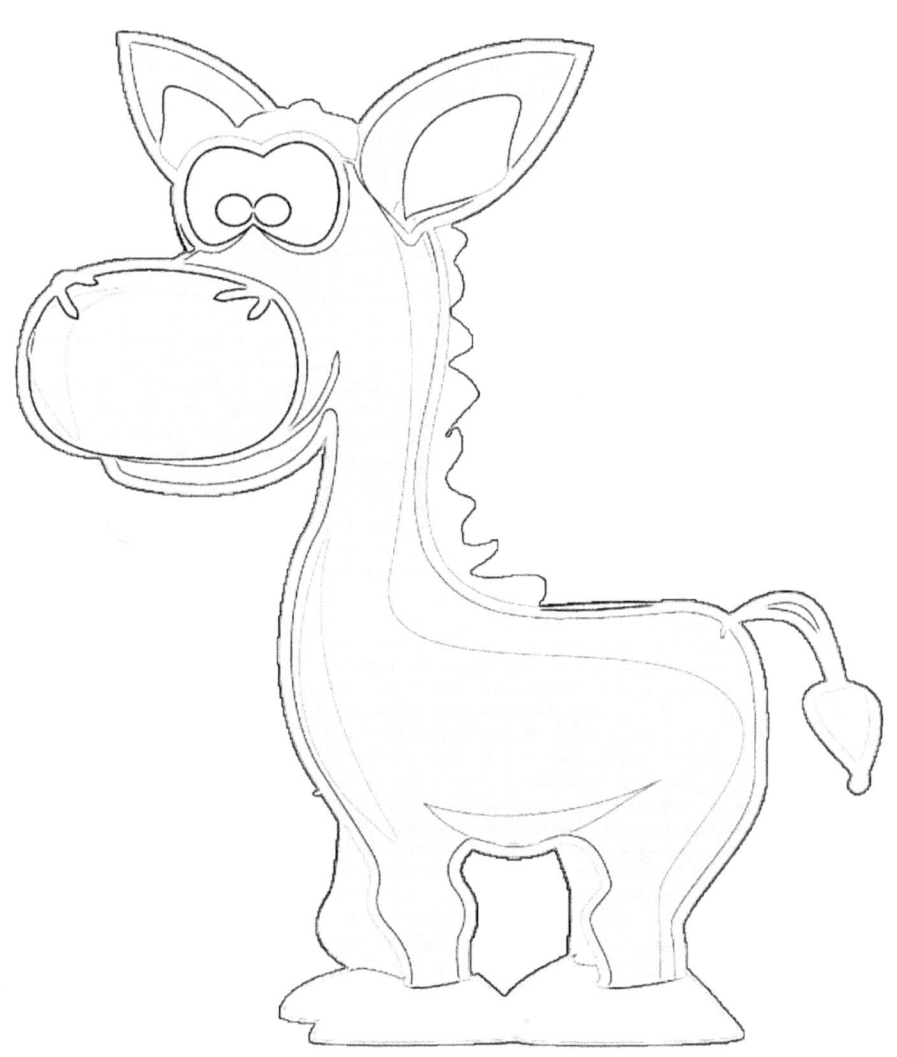

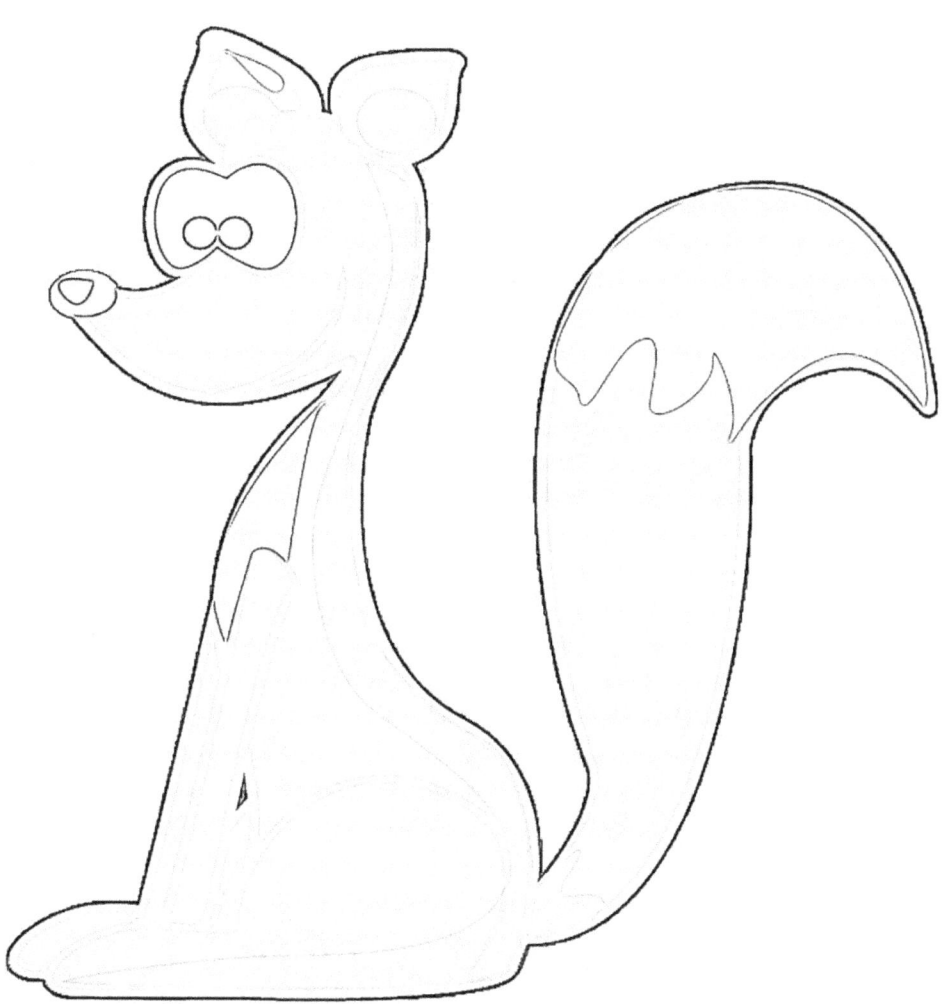

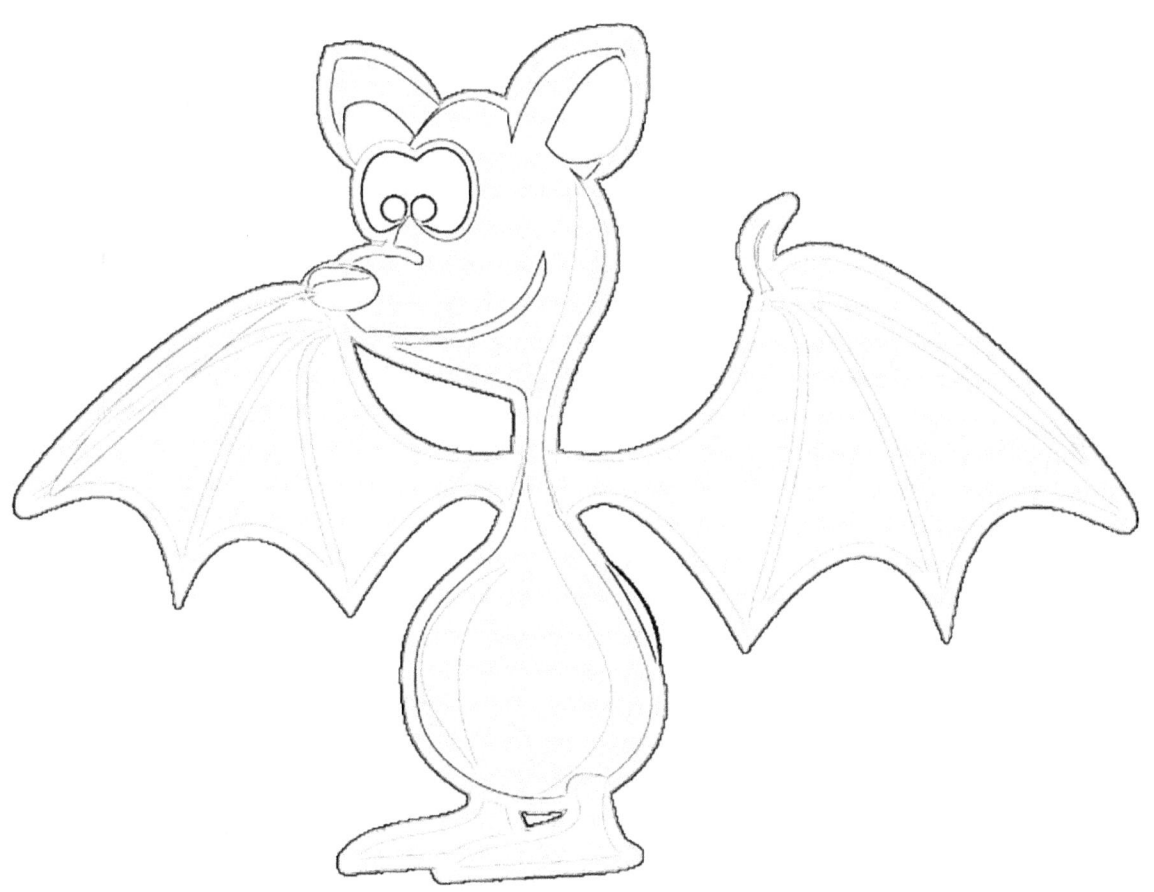

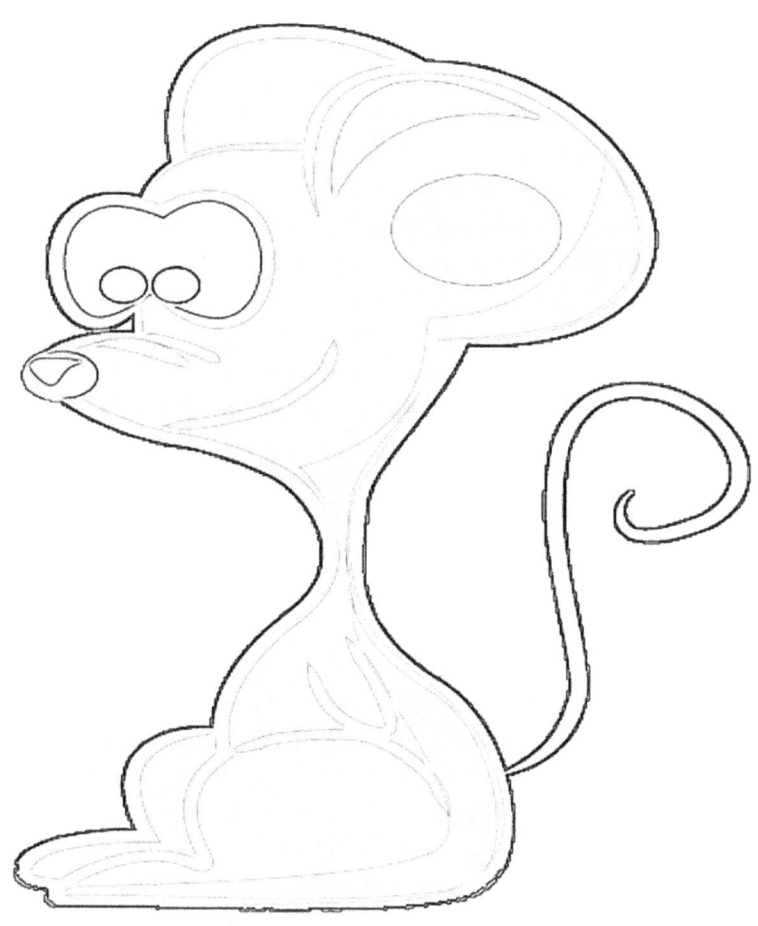

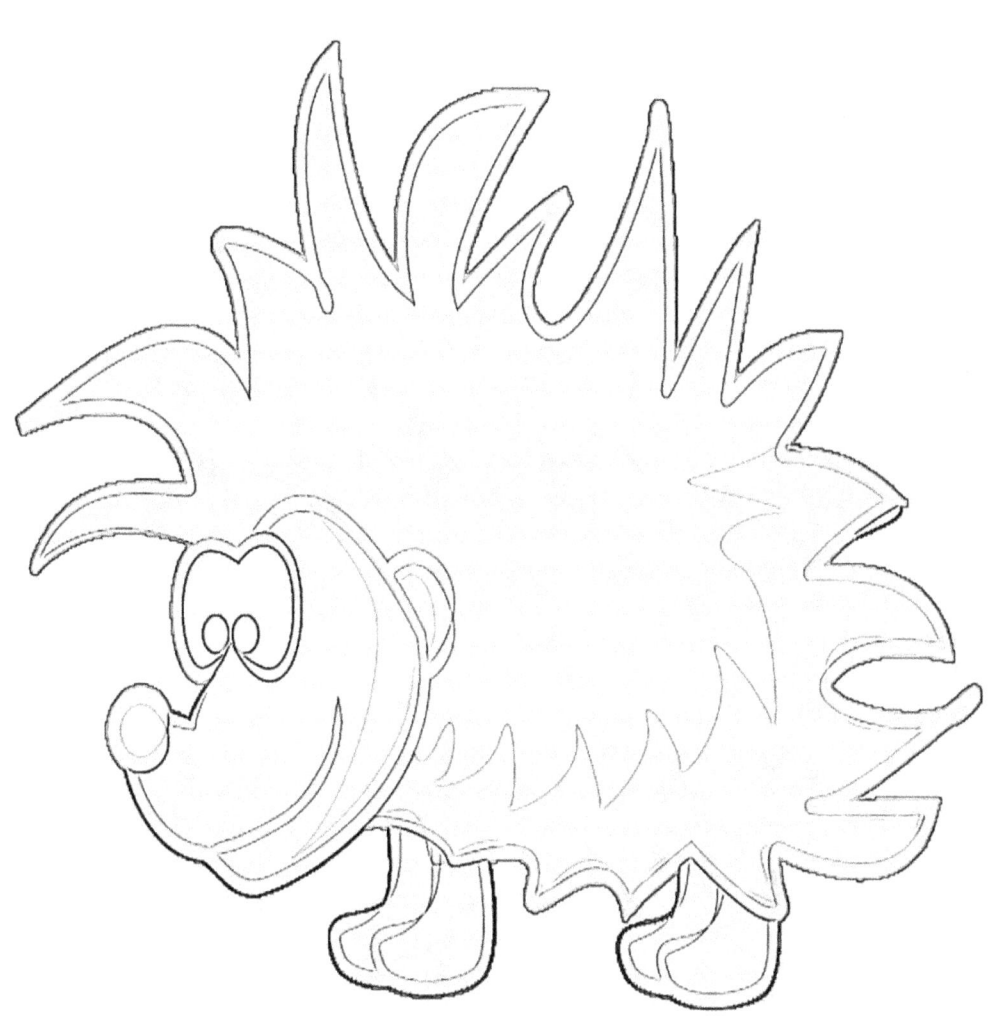

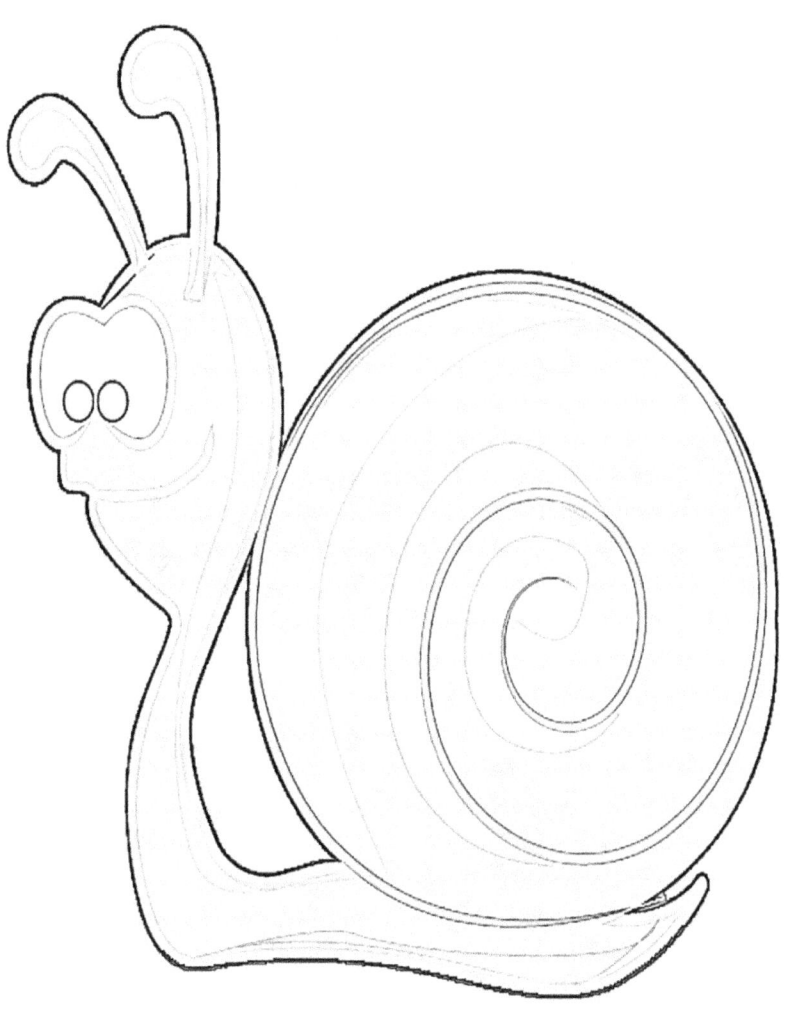

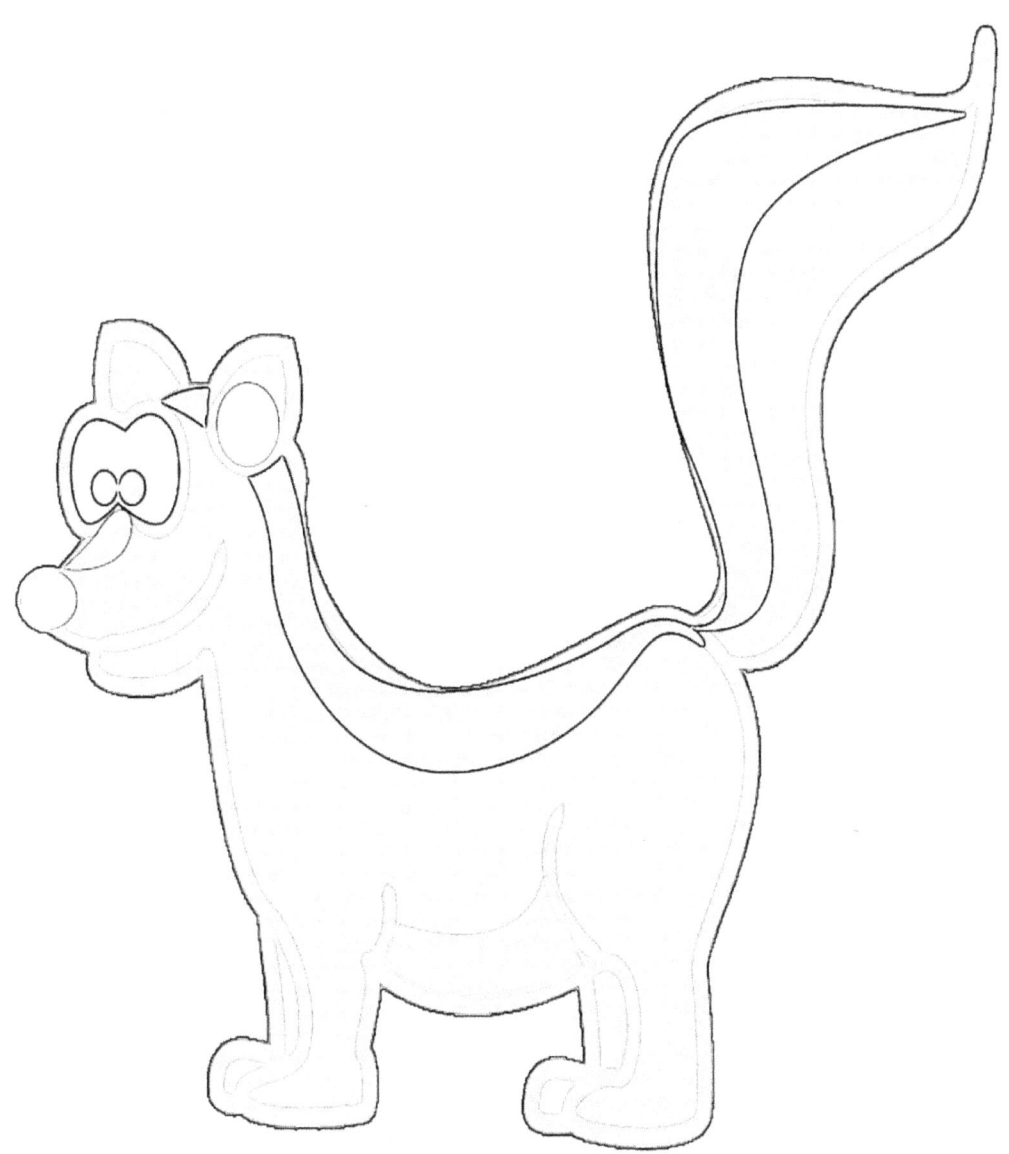

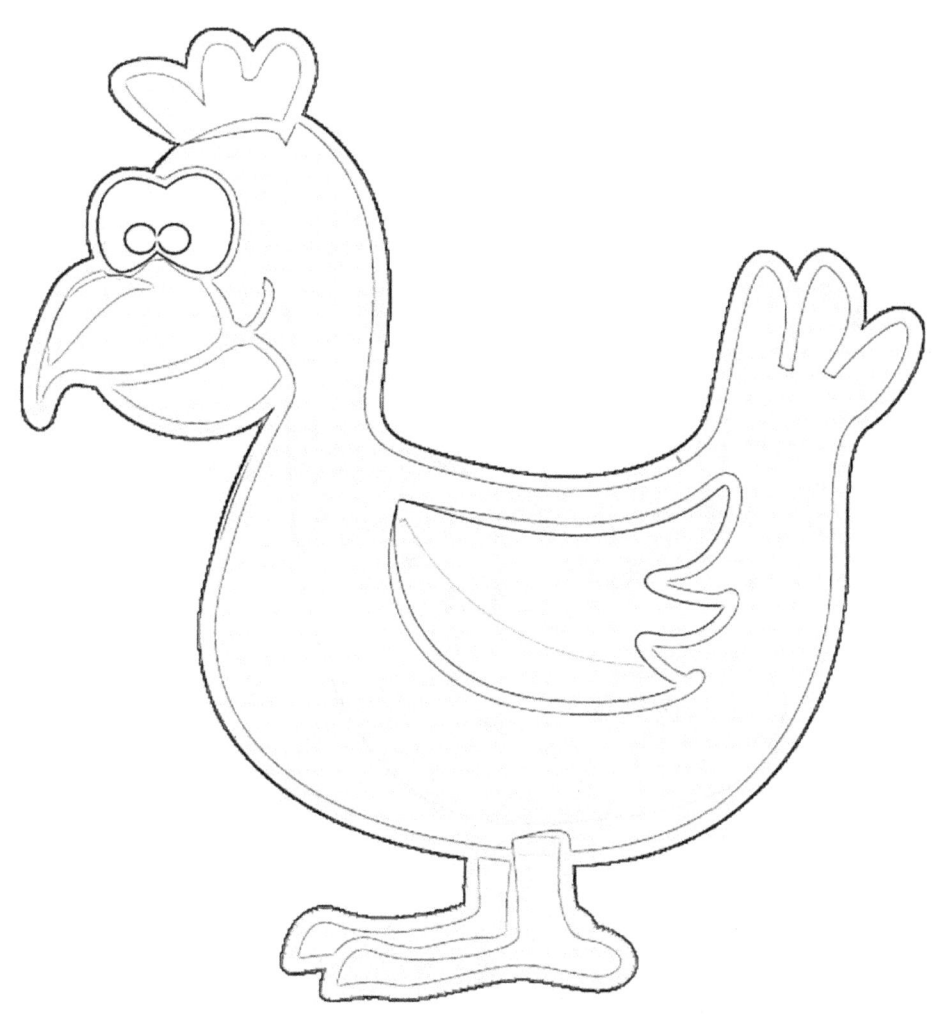

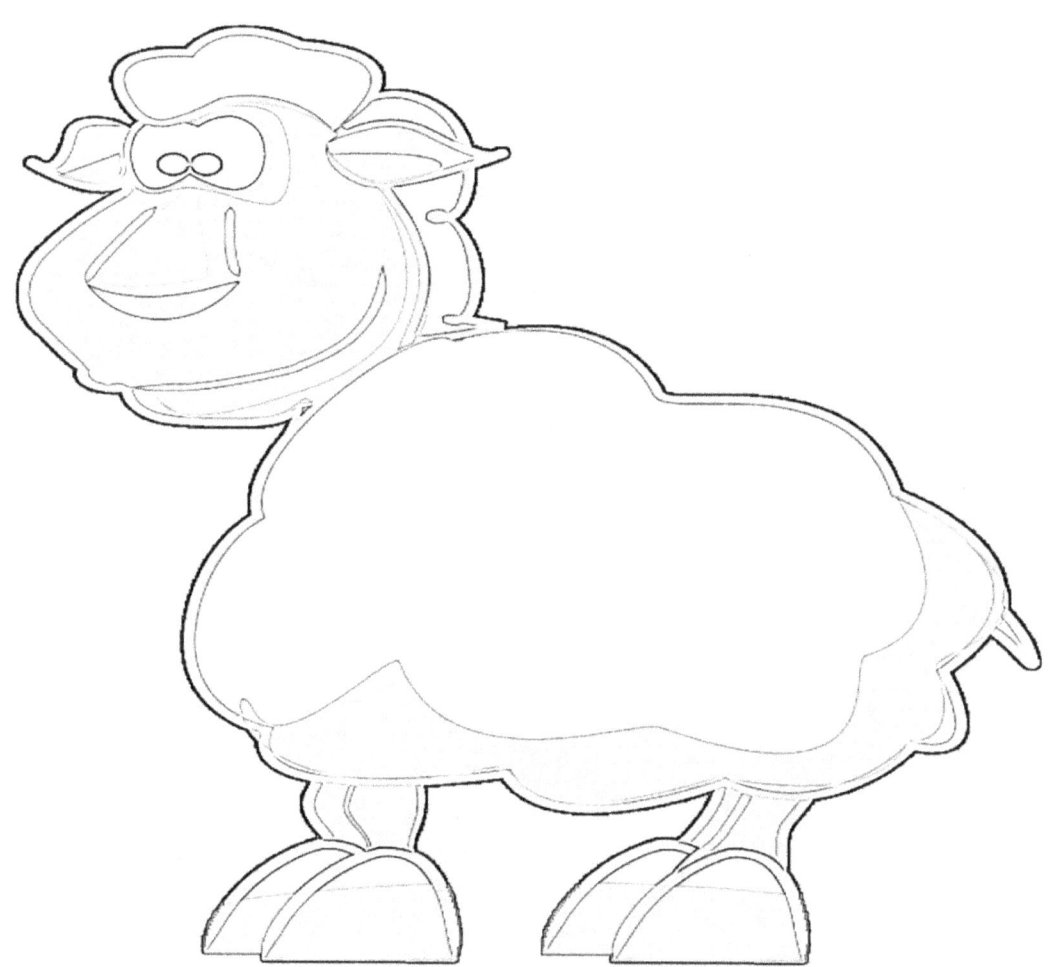

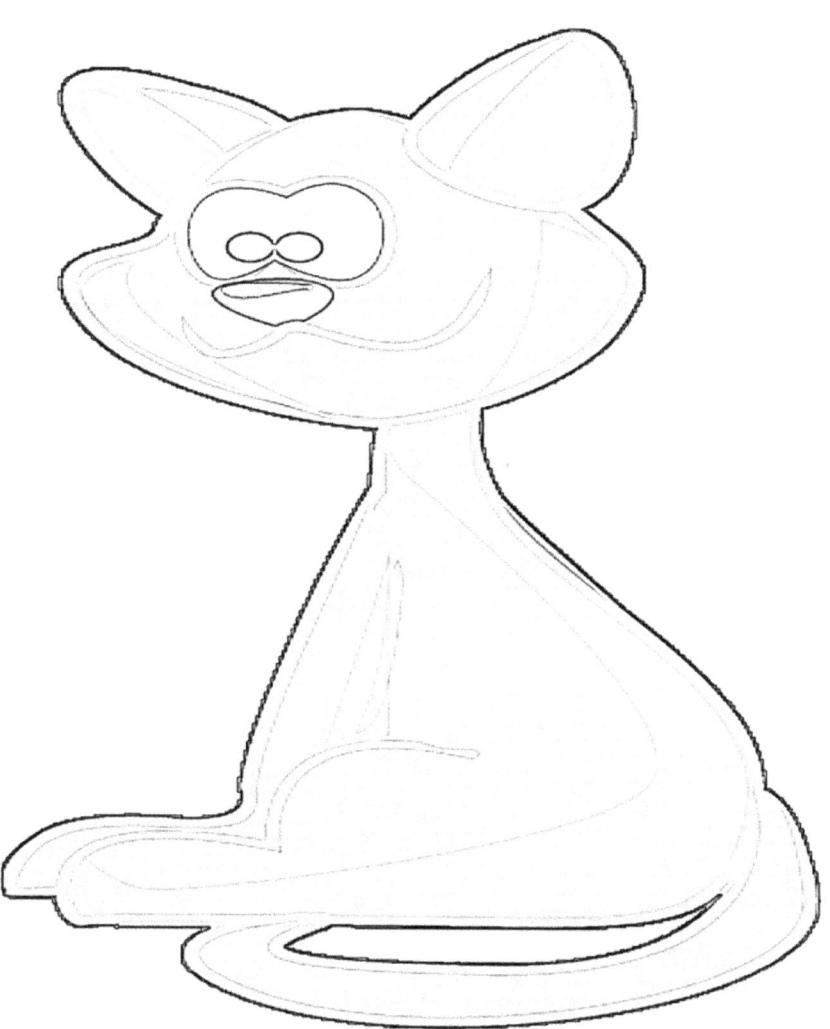

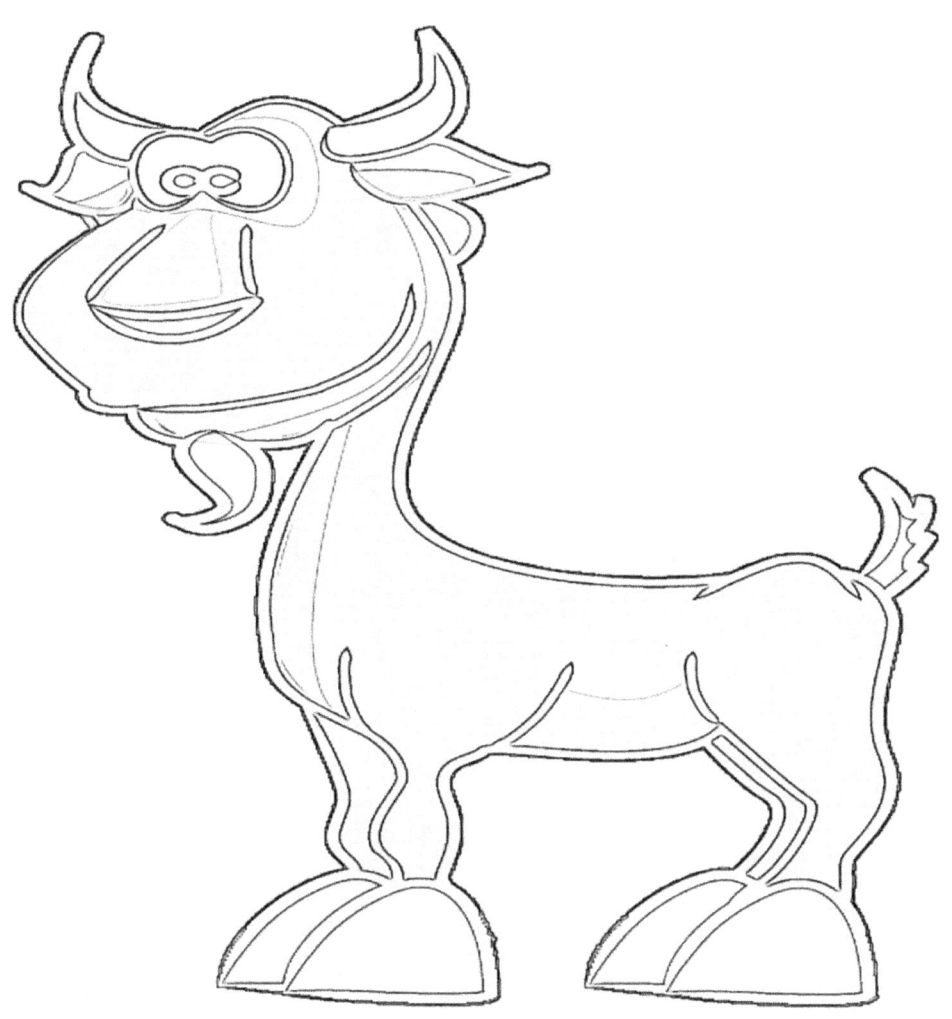

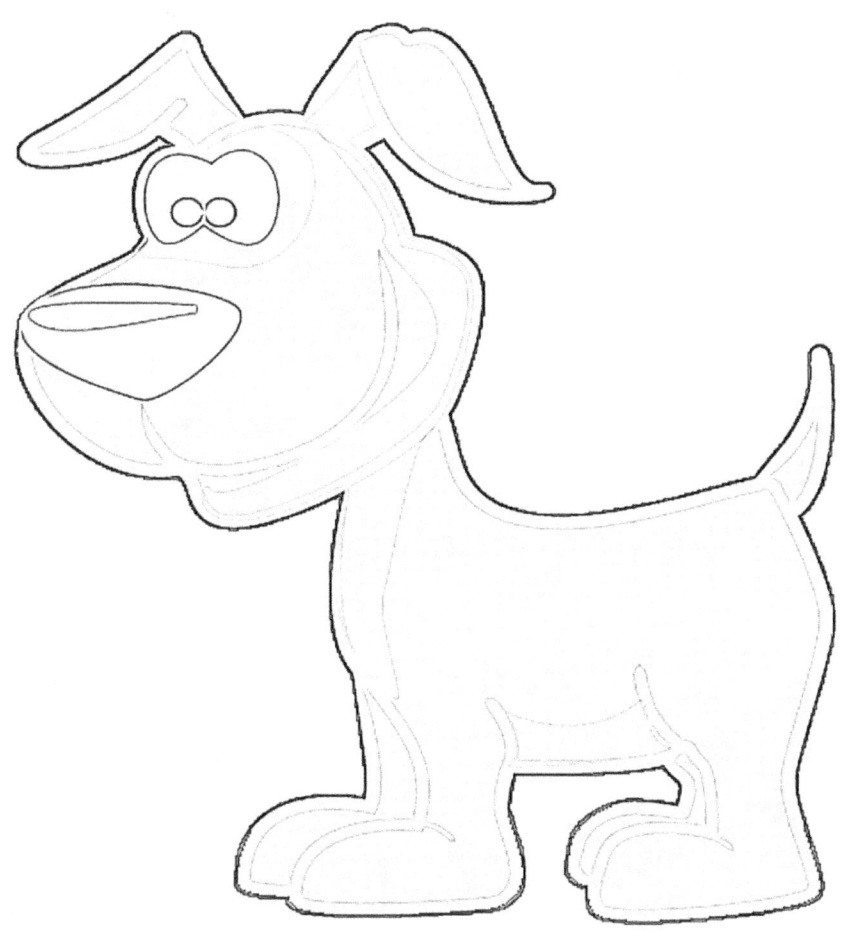

AMAZING ANIMALS
Coloring Book

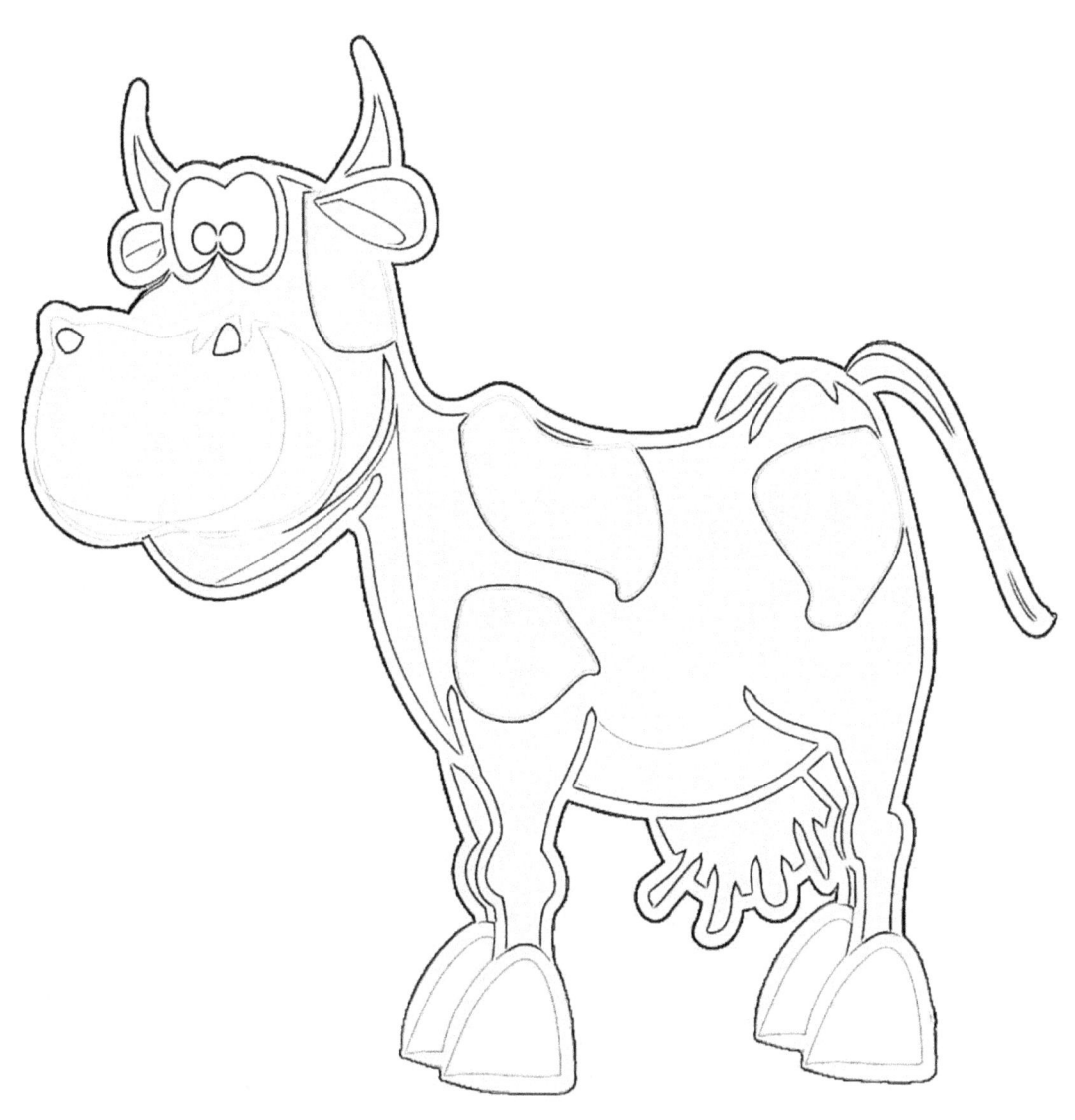

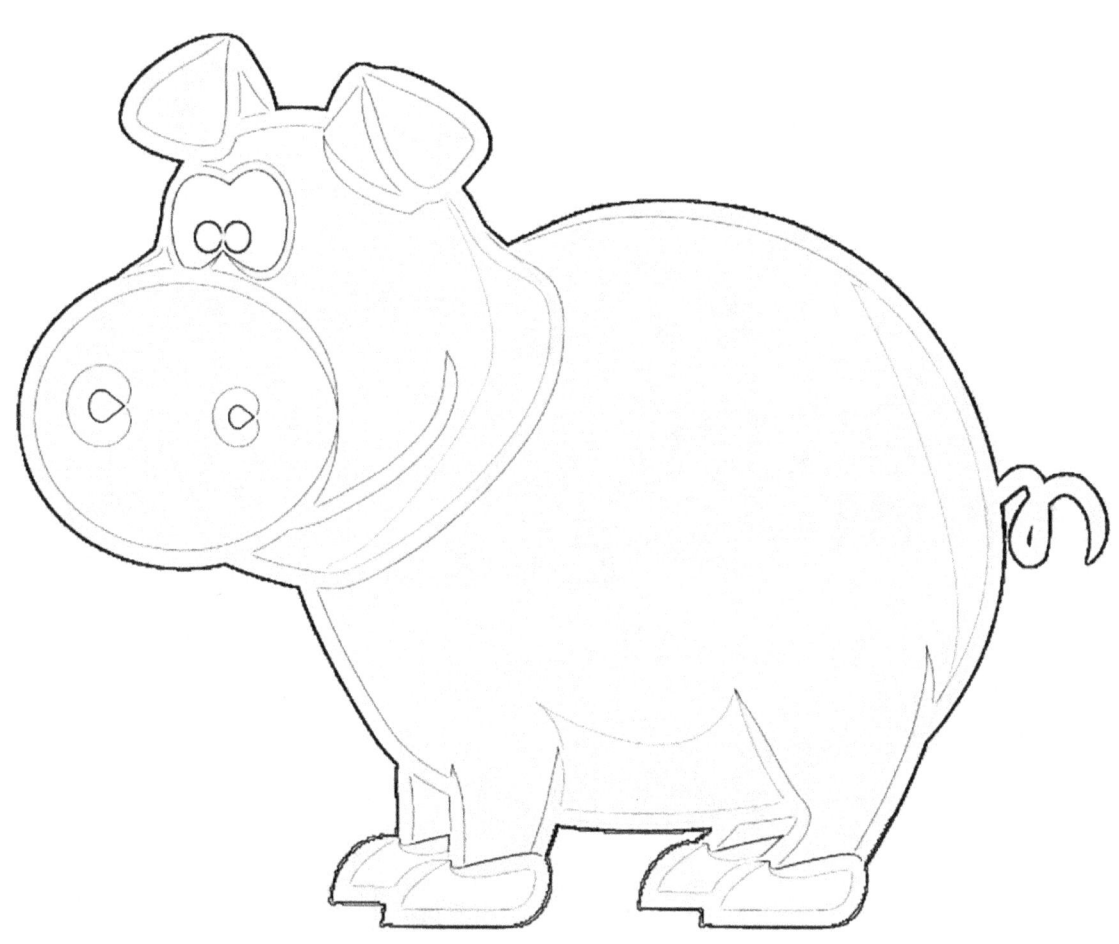

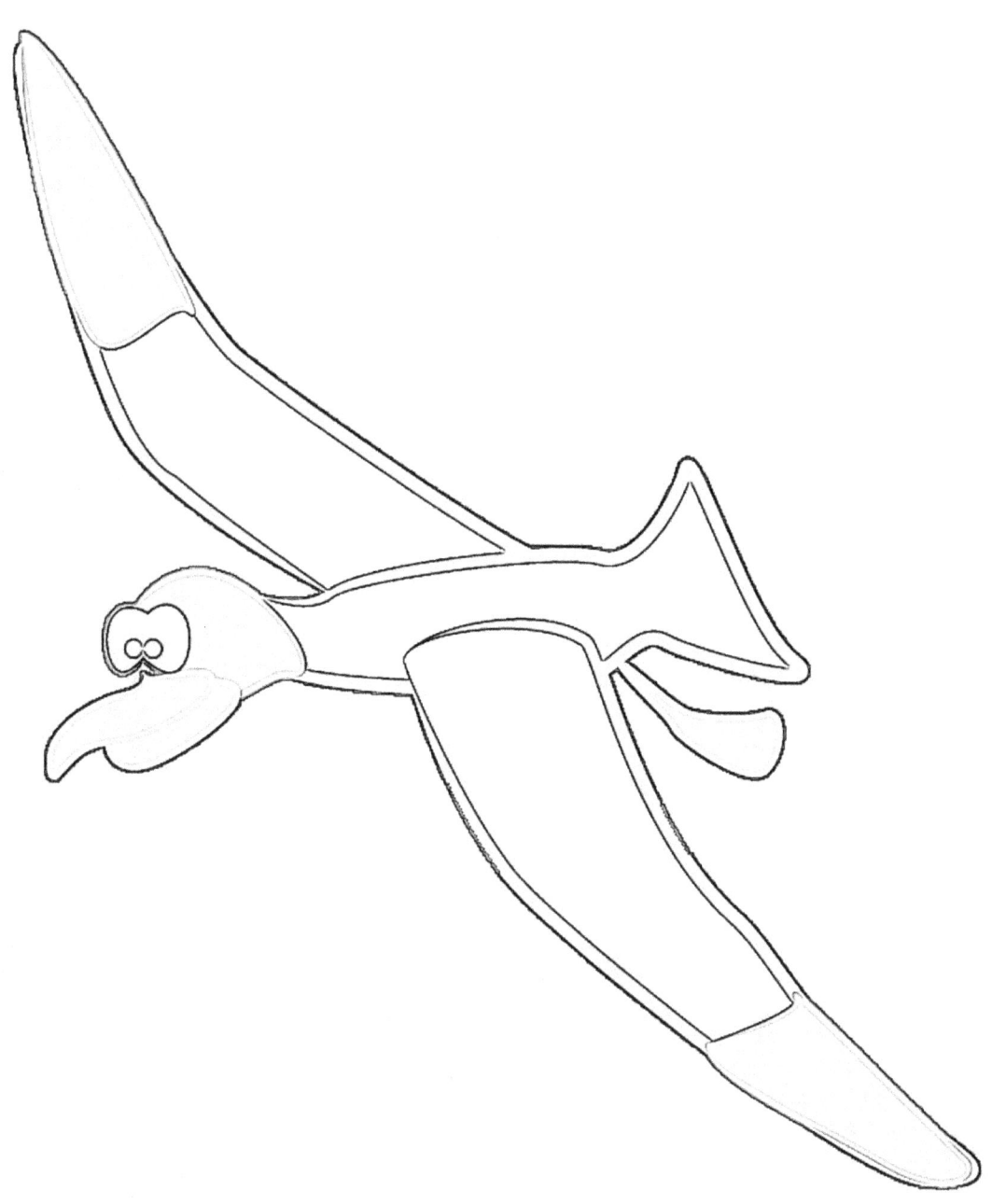

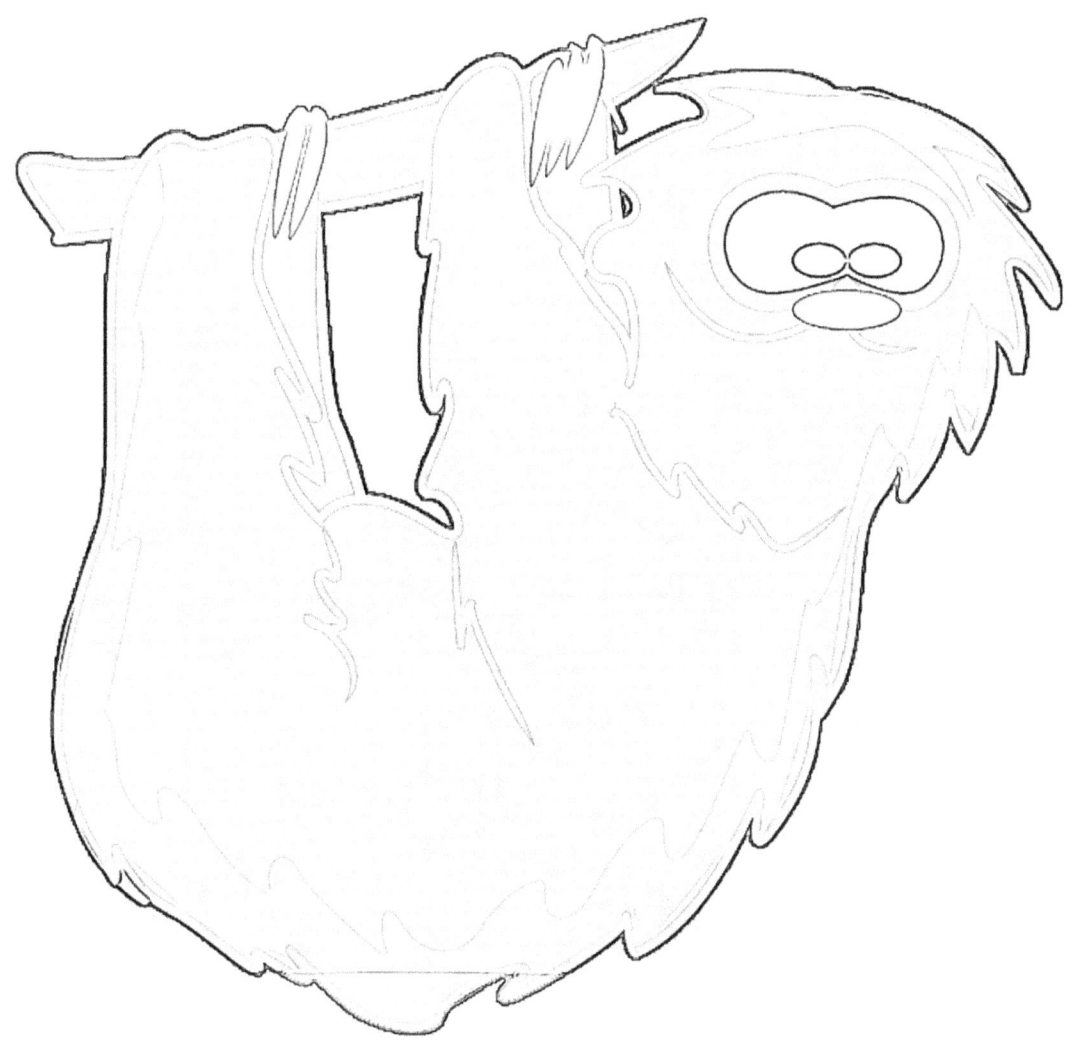

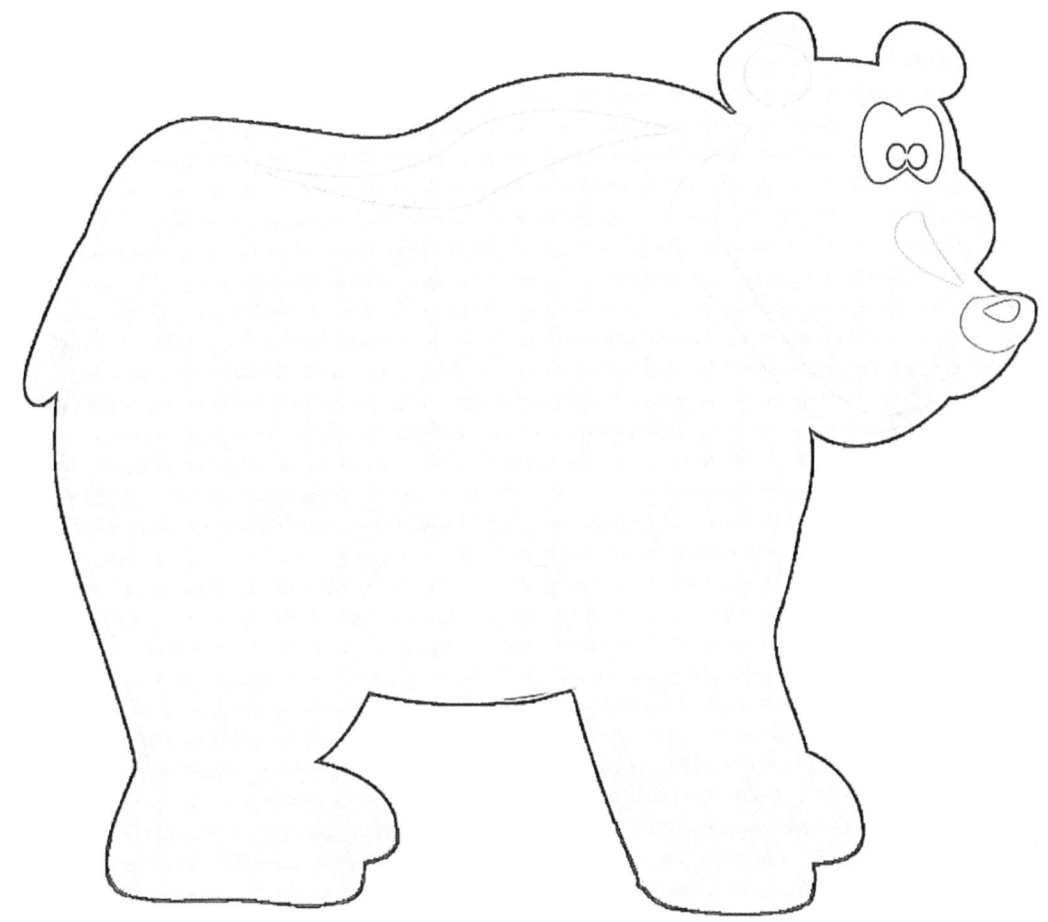

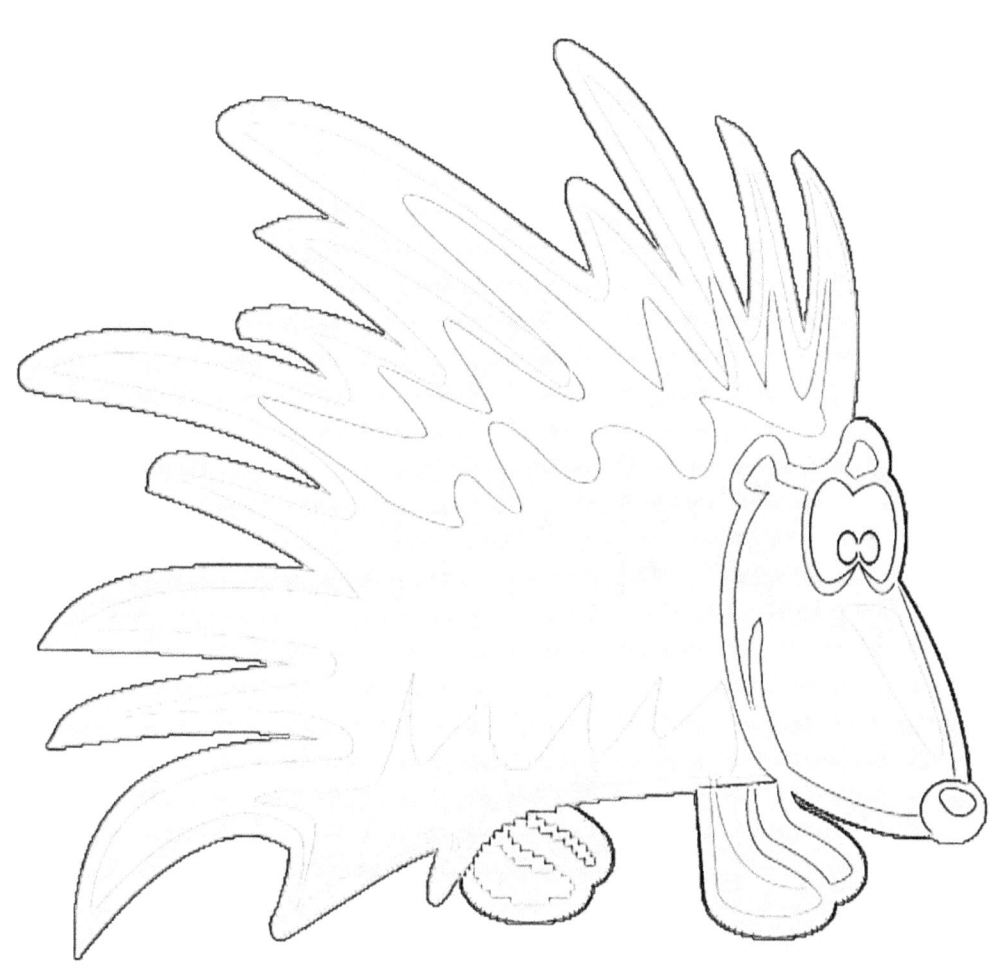

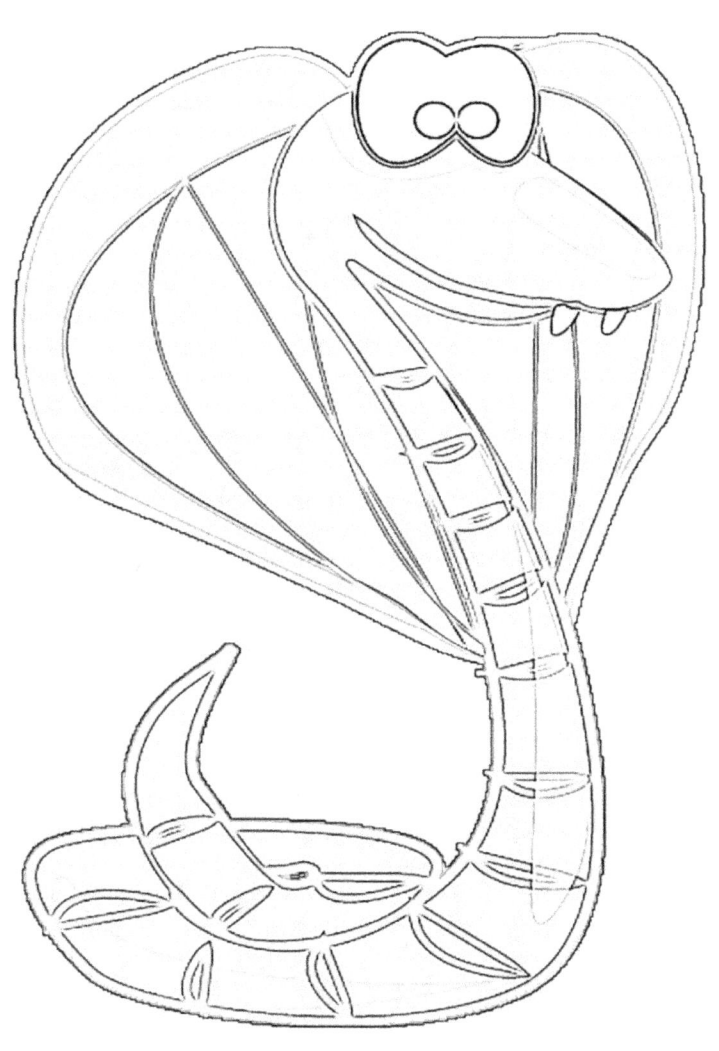

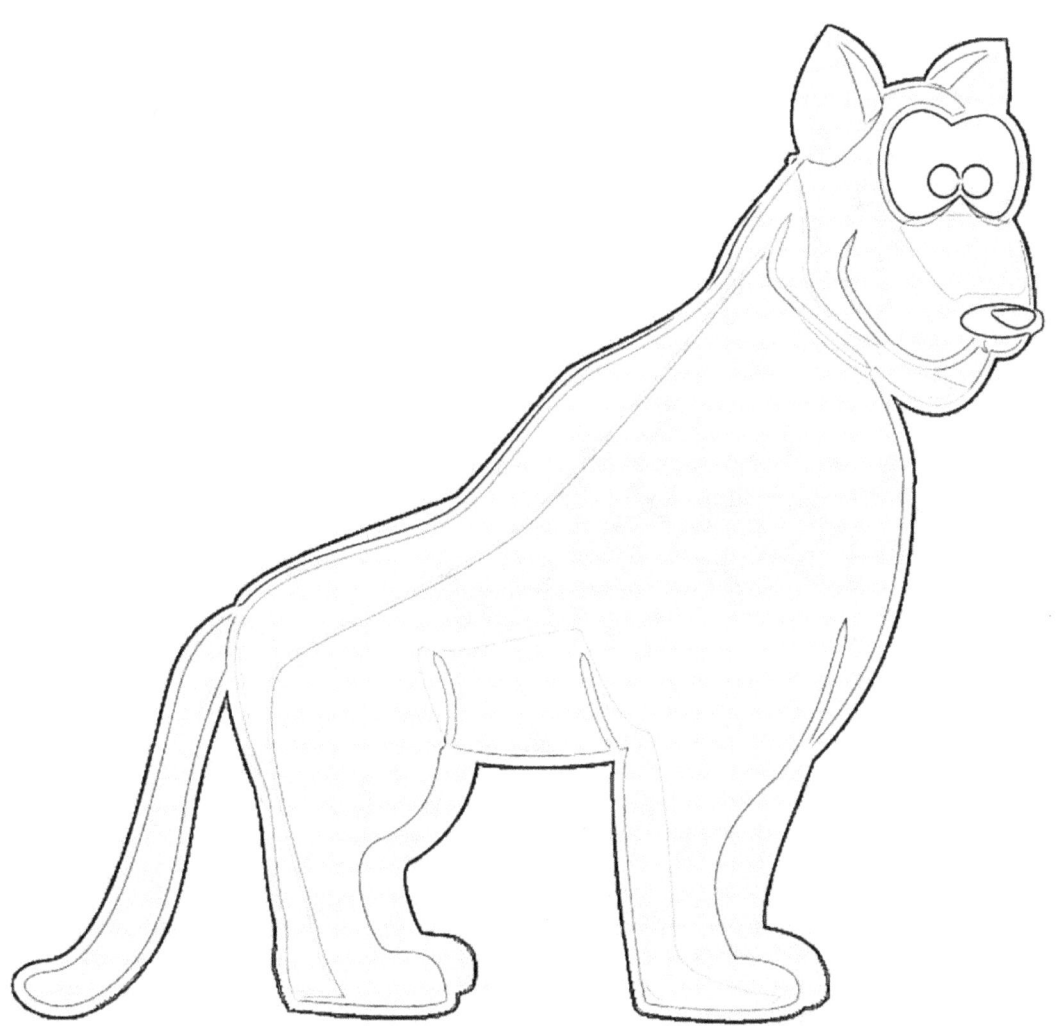

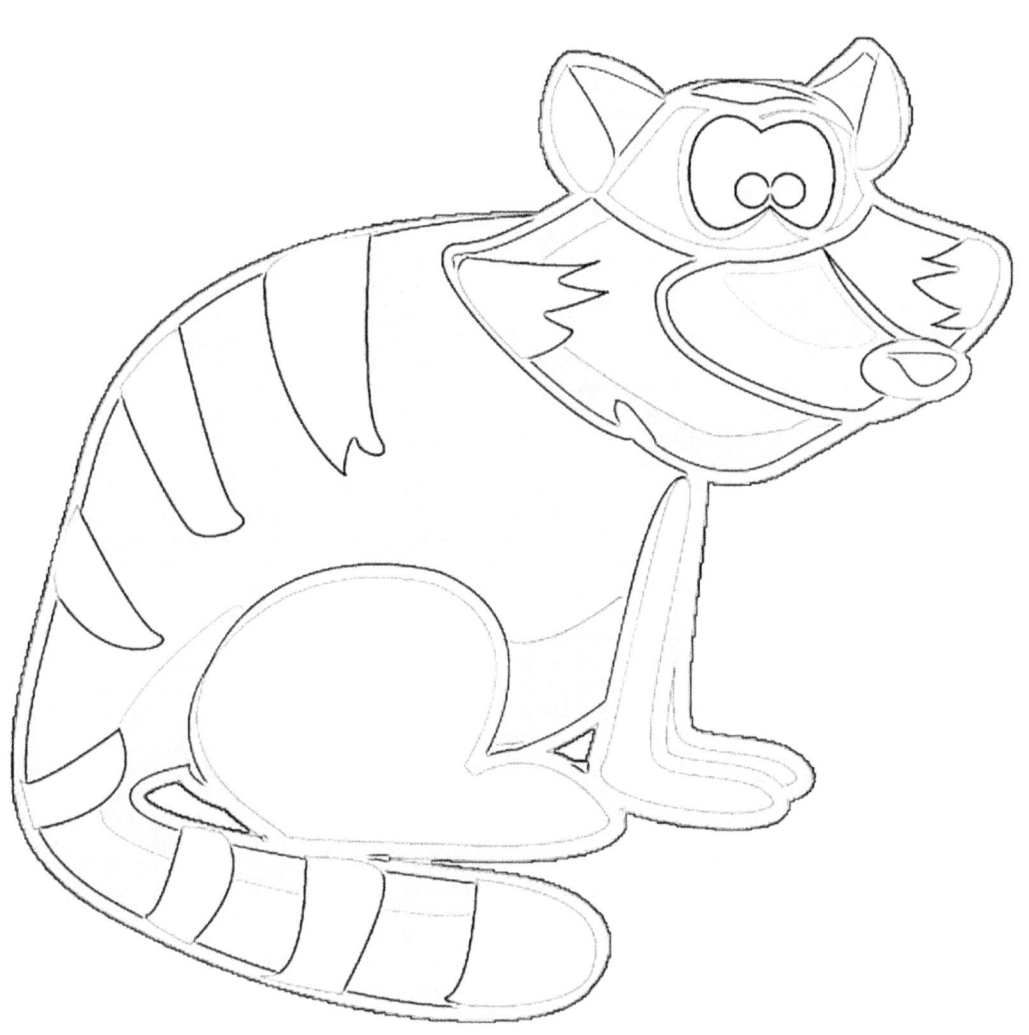

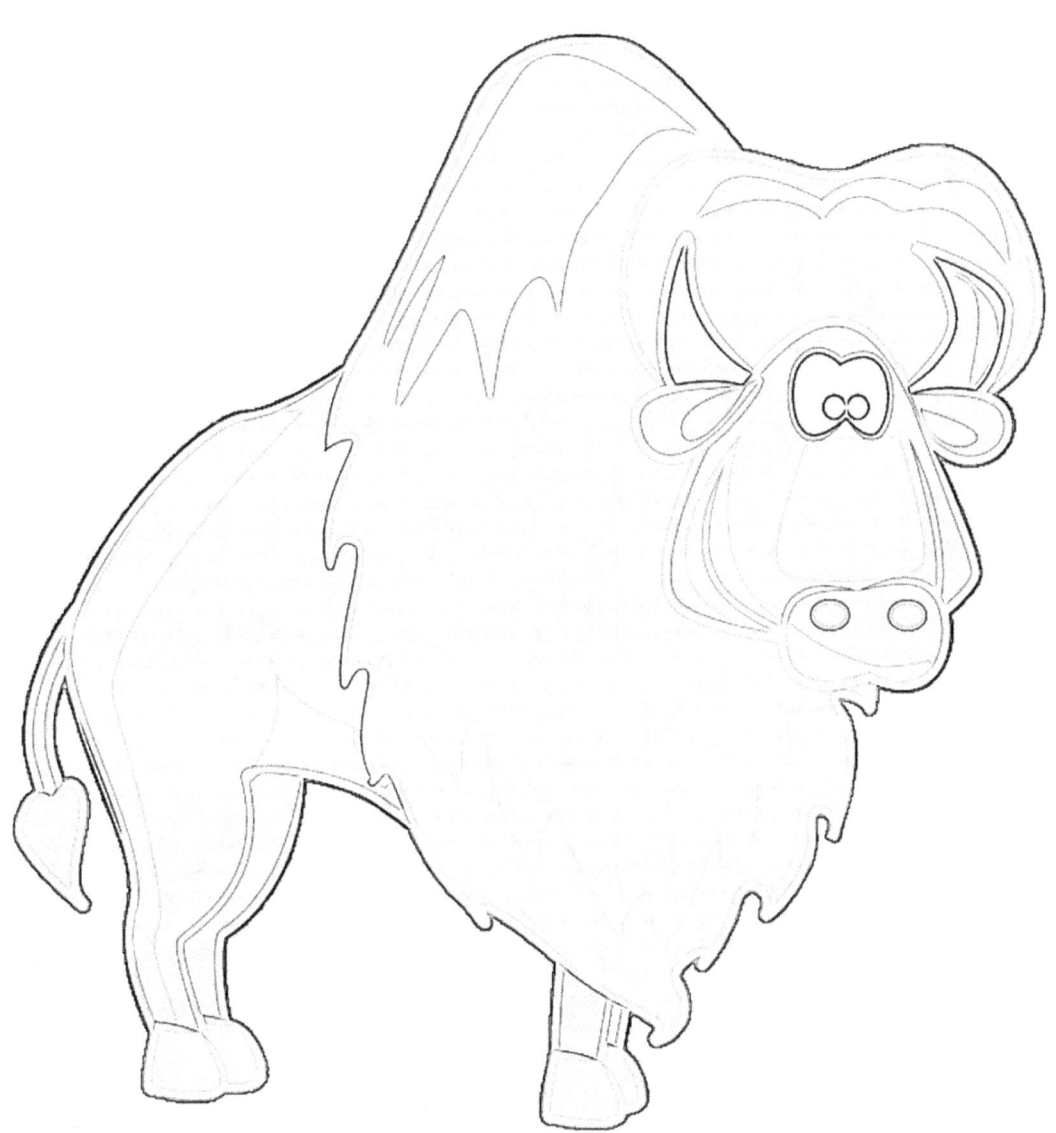

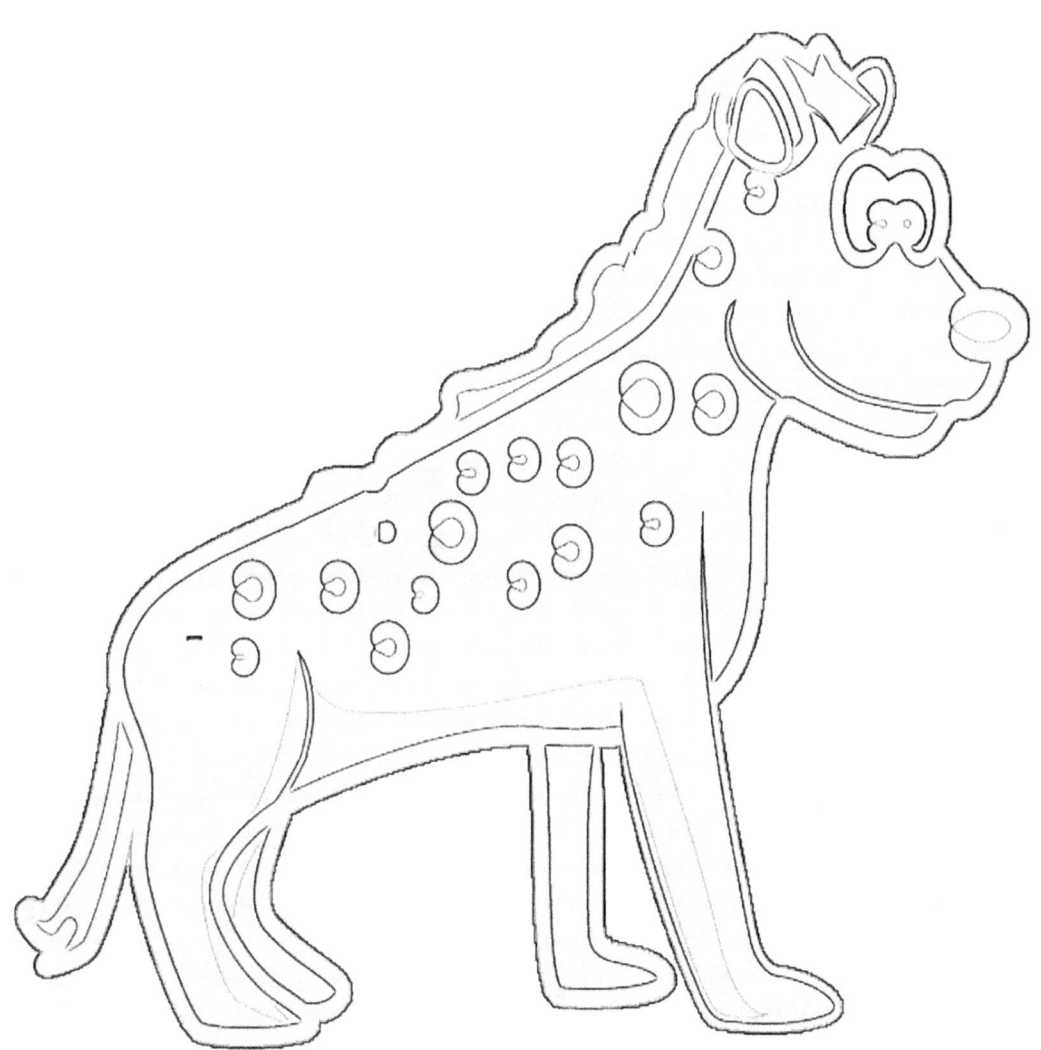

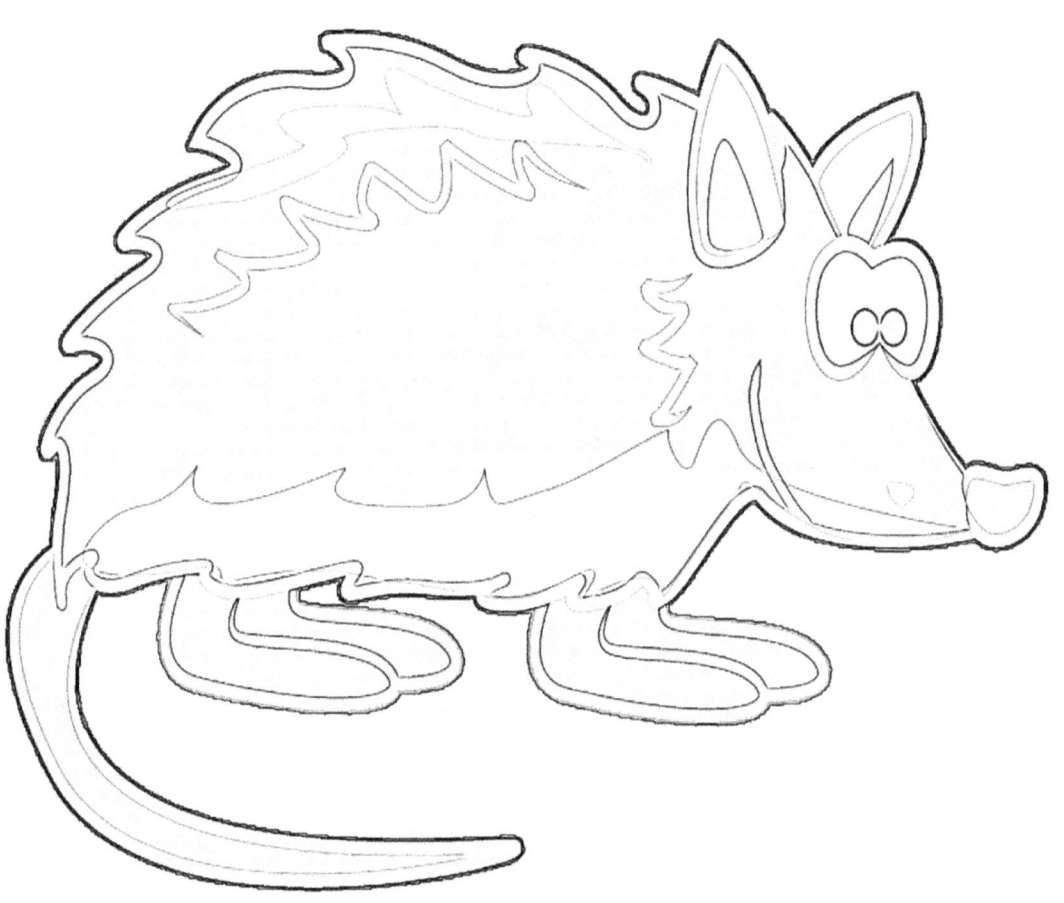

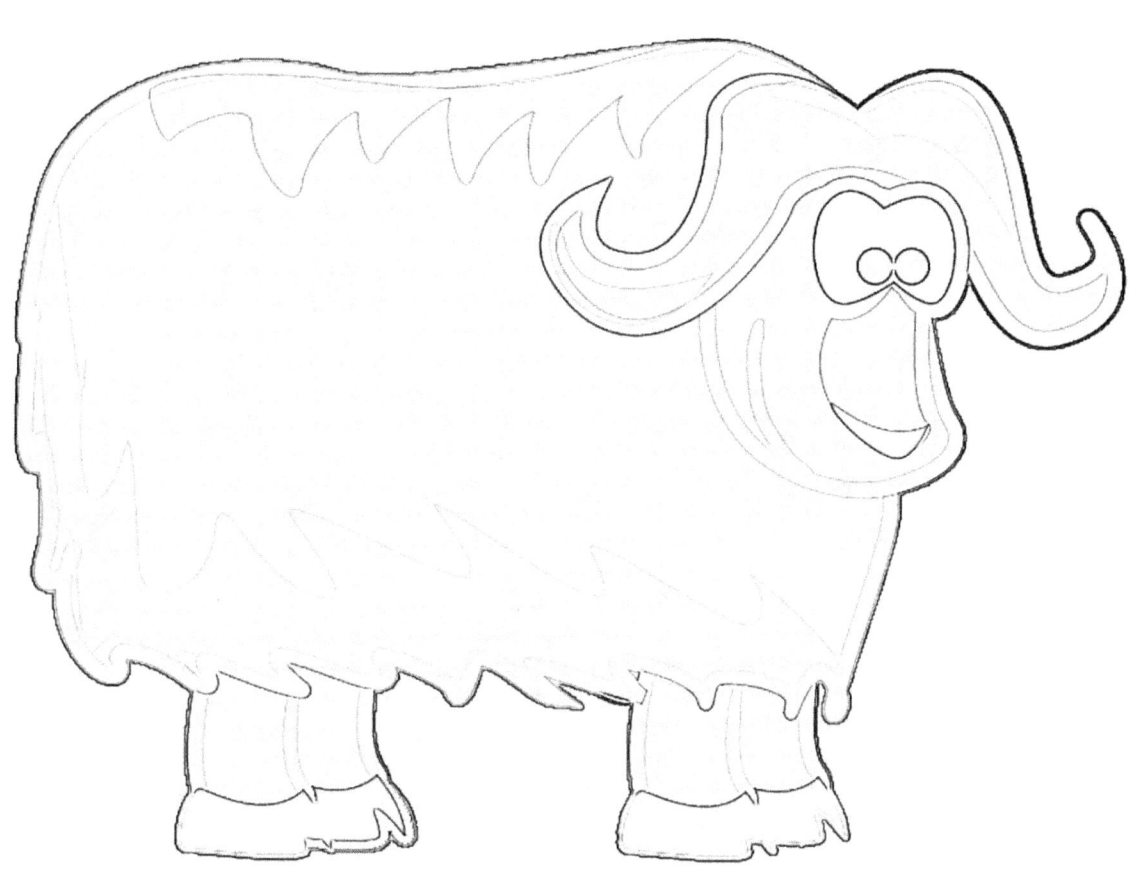

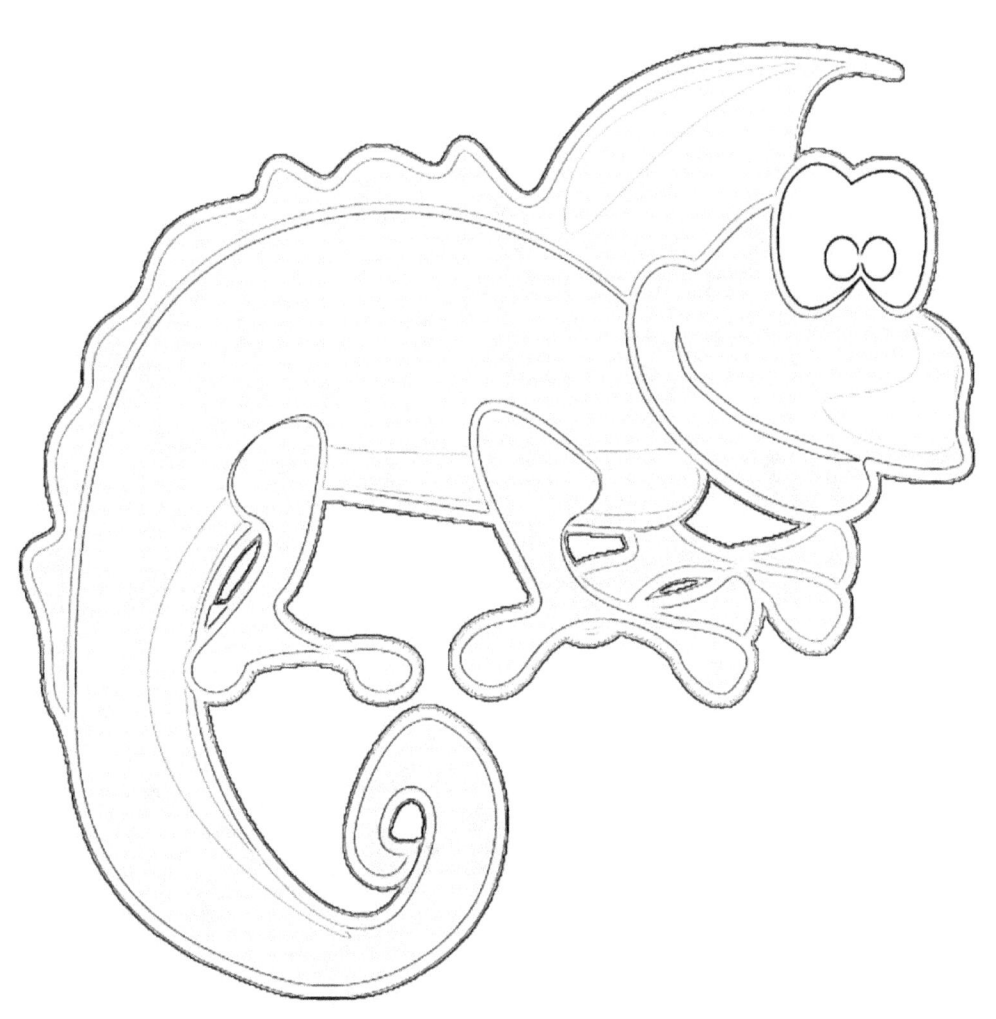

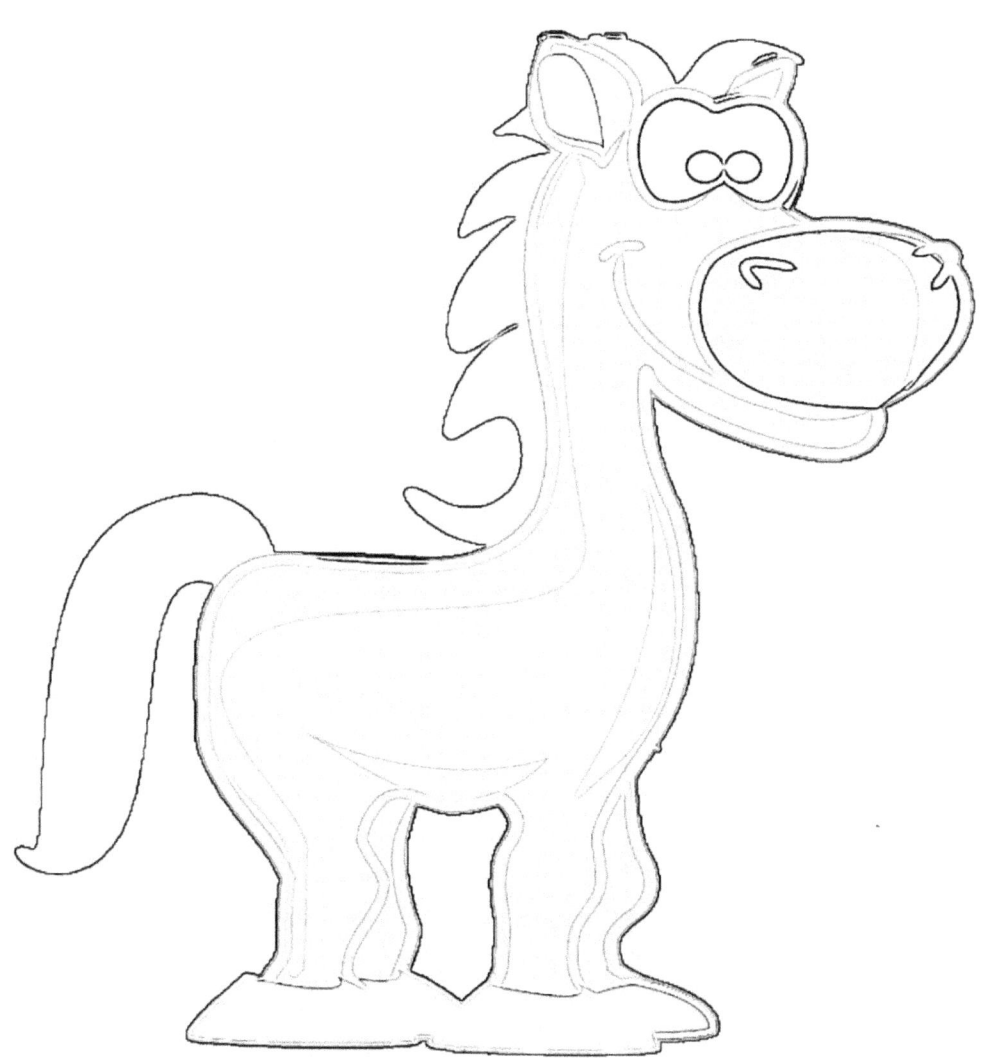

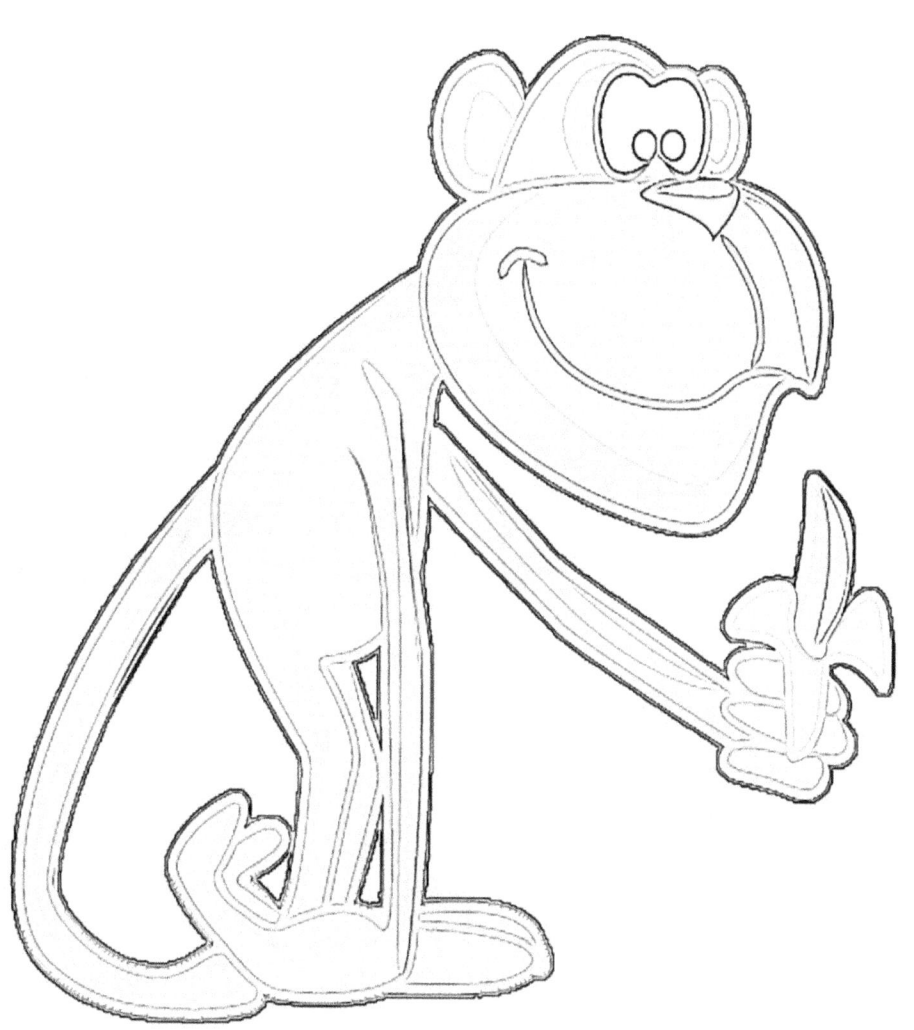

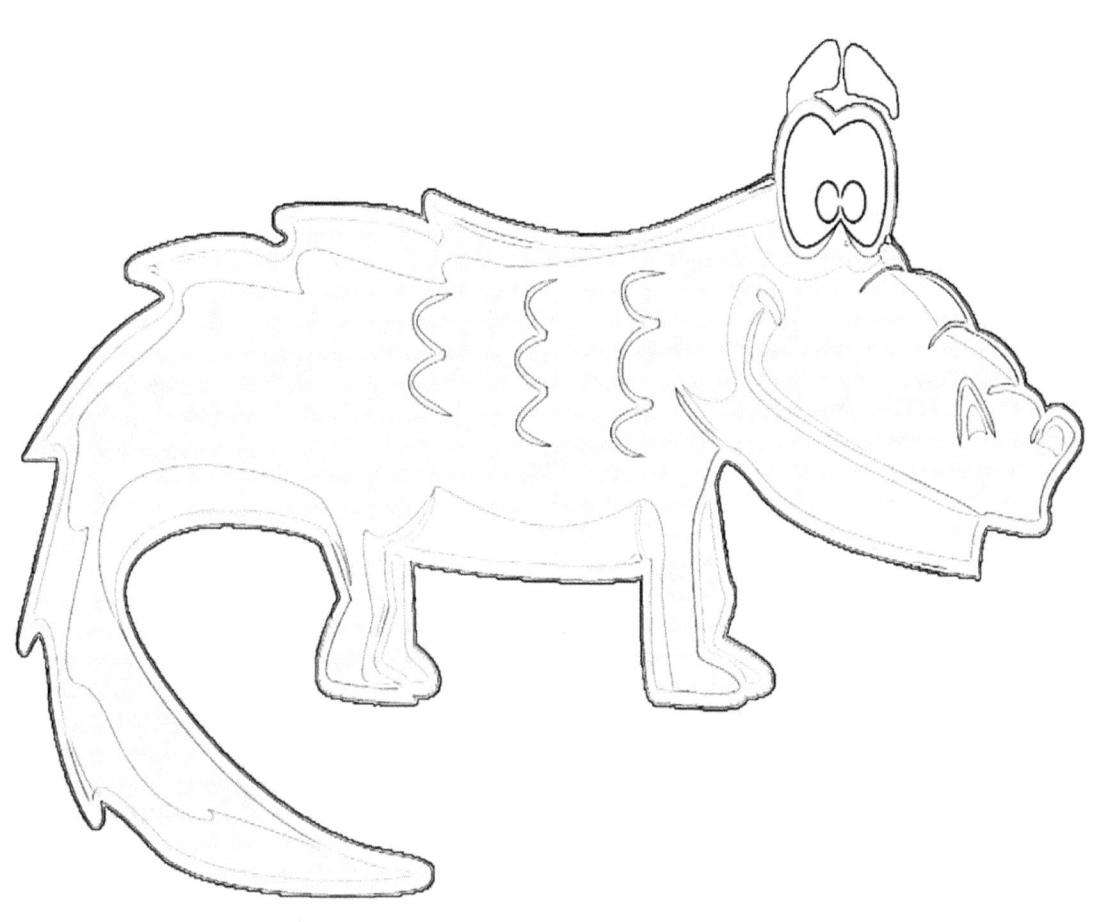

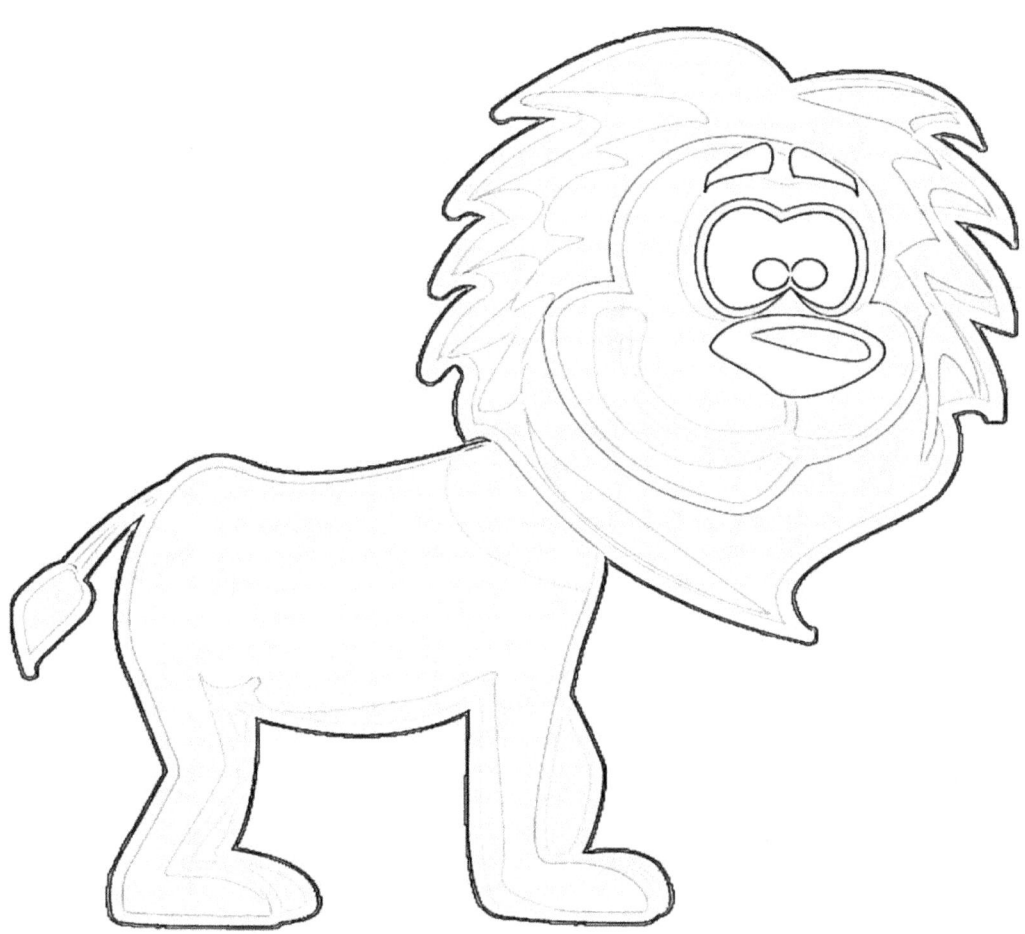

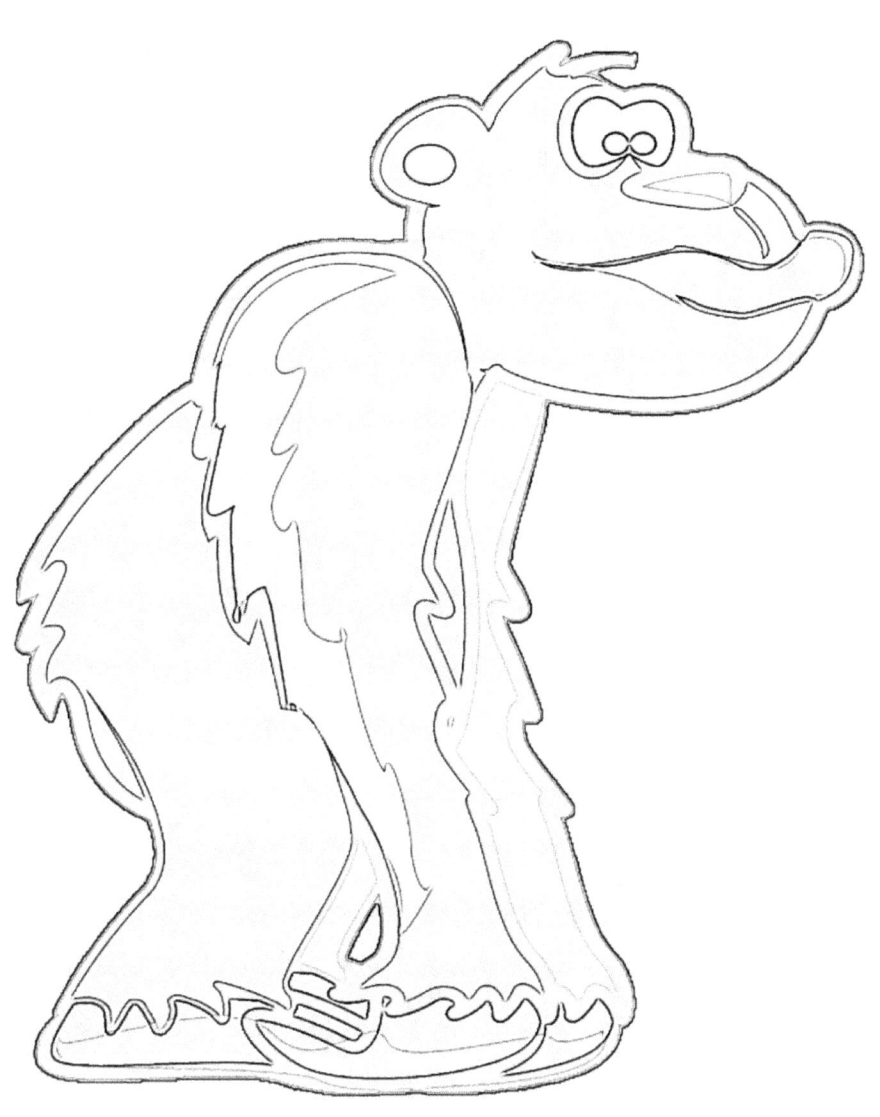

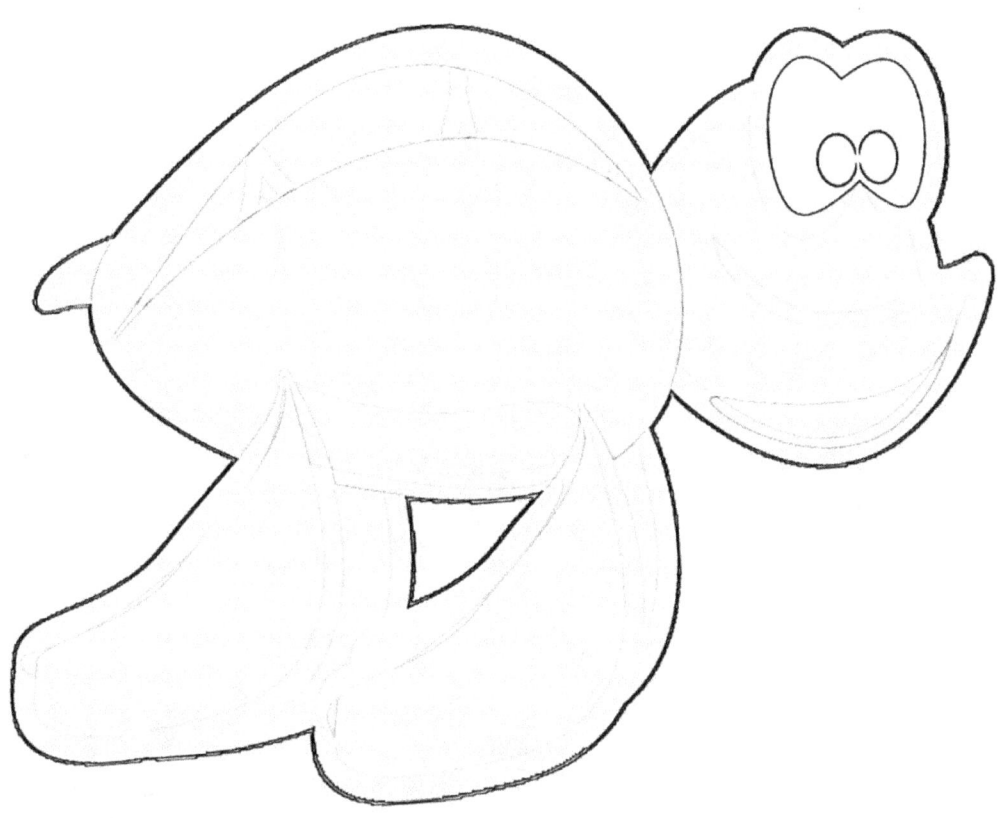

www.ingramcontent.com/pod-product-compliance
Lightning Source LLC
Chambersburg PA
CBHW081553170526
45166CB00009B/2690